Dividend Inve Simplified

The Step-by-Step Guide to Make Money and Create Passive Income in the Stock Market with Dividend Stocks

© **Copyright 2019 - All rights reserved.**

Table of Contents

Introduction

"Pioneering don't pay."

This quote from the renowned industrialist Andrew Carnegie is often the guiding principle followed by successful dividend investors.

There are many beginners in the stock market that are typically attracted by glamor instead of profits.

Just try to tell an average investor about a company that introduces "the next big thing", a terrific product upgrade, or a new acquisition of a popular brand, and you can easily capture their attention.

Try again to share some details about a blue-chip company that has recorded steady sales and has been increasing its dividend payouts, and they may start to yawn.

Contrary to what many stock market investors believe, glamorous innovation is not a reliable metric to predict the success of a company.

A recently launched startup tech company that is managed by young entrepreneurs and is still retaining all of its earnings is unlikely the best investment for your portfolio. Statistics show that 8 out of 10 new startups fail in the first 5 years in the business.

But hope is not all lost because if you are reading this book, there's a big chance that you want to stand out in the all-conforming landscape of the stock market.

You have chosen the right book if you are interested in the stock market, and you want to explore dividend investing.

People decide to buy stocks because they are curious about what's happening in what was previously known as "the rich man's world". In the past, only the members of high society are capable of participating in this lucrative yet highly volatile financial market.

But over the years, the stock market has been flooded with curious individuals who want to make money. Sure, there are stories of success, but there are also stories of people who have lost their investments.

Stock market investing is a risky financial venture because there are many variables that are not within your control. That is why as a beginner, you need to study the market well and use proven strategies that will help you achieve your financial objectives.

Now, if your goal is to create a steady stream of regular passive income while gradually growing your investment portfolio, then dividend investing might be right for you.

If you are really interested to make money without feeling too anxious about the high volatility in the stock market, then you should try to build a portfolio composed of companies that are paying regular dividends.

It will take time before you master the nuts and bolts of dividend investing, but the best time to start learning all about it is today.

The objective of this book is to help private individuals who want to learn the basics of dividend investing. In this book, you will be able to:

- Understand the benefits and drawbacks of investing in dividend stocks

- Learn the terminology in stock dividend investing

- Consider the different factors you need before you invest in dividend stocks

- Explore the different strategies used by successful dividend investors

- Follow specific steps in conducting company due diligence

- And a whole lot more!

So, if you are ready to learn all about dividend investing, let's get started!

Chapter 1 - Earning Passive Income through Dividend Investments

"The best time to plant a tree was 20 years ago. The second-best time to plant a tree is today." - Chinese Proverb

If you are looking for an investment that provides regular passive income, stock dividend investing might be right for you.

Many public companies are regularly distributing a portion of their profits to stockholders. Most of them are paying their investors a certain amount, and there are also other companies that gradually increase their payouts.

Are All Publicly Listed Companies Paying Dividends?

Not all companies listed on the stock market are paying dividends. Some choose to share their profits to their shareholders mainly to attract more public investments, while other companies choose not to pay any dividend and instead allocate all their earnings to grow the business.

For established companies with regular profit streams and don't need a lot of reinvestments, paying dividends is ideal because of the following reasons:

- Many stock investors are attracted to buy stocks of public companies who are paying dividends.

- Paying regular dividends is one indicator that a company is strong. It is usually a good indicator that the company has positive predictions for profits in the future, which makes the stock more appealing. Take note that a higher demand for stocks will likely lead to an increased price.

Publicly listed companies in the US that are issuing regular dividend payouts include Microsoft (MSFT), Verizon (VZ), Exxon Mobil (XOM), Apple (AAPL), and Wells Fargo (WFC).

Some public companies, on the other hand, decide not to issue regular dividend payouts because of various reasons such as:

- Corporate directors believe the company will do a better job of increasing shareholder value through reinvestments

- Companies are avoiding the expensive charges for new stock issuance, so they choose not to raise funds through this method, and they decide not to share the profits

- Companies who decide to temporarily defer the dividend payouts to start a new project, buy another company, or buy back some of their stocks

- Startups that are growing at a rapid rate and choose not to issue payouts because they have to invest in their growth

Bear in mind that the decision to start issuing dividend payouts or to increase the present dividend payout rate is a major business decision.

It seems enticing for a company to share its profits to its shareholders, but it should consider the sustainability of the practice. Companies who suddenly suspend or even decrease its payout rate could be interpreted as a bad signal.

Publicly listed companies in the US that are not paying dividends include Facebook (FB), Alphabet Inc (GOOGL), Amazon (AMZN), Biogen (BIIB), and Tesla (TSLA).

What Are the Types of Dividend Payouts?

A dividend payout refers to the cash or stocks issued by a company to its shareholders. Take note that not all types of payouts are in the form of cash. Some companies choose to issue new stocks, or even in the form of properties. Here are the differences between these types of dividend payouts:

Cash Dividends

Most companies who pay dividends issue them in the form of a check or recently, via electronic transfer. The equivalent value of the cash payout will be transferred by the company to an individual investor account.

One important aspect to take note of cash dividends is the economic value transfer. Whenever a company issues cash dividends, there will be a loss in the price of the stock.

For example, if Verizon issues cash dividends equivalent to 5% of the share price, then the VZ stocks in NASDAQ will decrease by 5%.

Another aspect to consider is the taxation on the distribution value. Those who receive cash payouts are obliged to pay tax on the distribution value. This can further decrease the final value of the stocks.

Cash dividends are primarily beneficial for individual investors because it provides regular passive income aside from the capital appreciation of the stock holdings.

Stock Dividends

Some companies issue dividend payouts but not in the form of cash but instead in the form of stocks.

If you are interested in this type of dividend payout, you should take note that stock dividends are issued to company shareholders without prejudice.

Stock dividends are usually common stocks. If a company decides to release less than 25% of its total number of outstanding shares, then the payout is considered as stock dividends.

Meanwhile, the payout is considered as a stock split if the payout is higher than the outstanding shares.

When a company decides to release a 5% stock dividend, it must also increase the number of shares by 5%. If you own shares of that company, you will receive 1 share for every 20 shares you hold. If you hold 1 million shares, then you can receive 50,000 additional stocks.

But this transaction cannot increase the value of the company. When the share price of the company is $20, then its value will be $20 million.

After the release of the dividend payout in the form of stocks, the value of the company will stay the same. However, the share price will be lower because of the economic transfer of value.

The beauty of choosing dividend stocks is that you can have a choice. You could either retain your stocks and put your trust that the company will use the investment to further boost shareholder value, or you may choose to sell some of your stocks so you can convert them into cash.

Which One Is Better? Cash Dividend or Stock Dividend?

At first, many investors are more enticed with cash dividends mainly because you can get tangible returns from your stock investments instead of waiting for years for your shares to appreciate.

However, there are also advantages to choosing stock dividends over cash dividends.

In different ways, it is better for both the company and the shareholder to choose stock dividends.

For investors, there is no need to pay tax upon receipt of stock dividends. Companies, on the other hand, can forge stronger relationships with investors who acquire more shares through the stock dividend payouts.

Stock experts agree that stock dividends are considered better than cash dividends as long as they are not bundled with a cash option. Remember, you can convert the shares into cash or choose to keep it for future profit. If you opt for the cash dividend, you virtually have no other option.

So, is cash payout not a good choice? It depends. If you want instant payout, then the cash dividend is the way to go. But if you want more choices with your dividend, stock dividends are way better. Also, you can still decide to reinvest your cash dividends into the company through a reinvestment plan.

Choosing stock dividends is not always a better choice. The stock market is extremely volatile, and your stock investments may be affected by economic downturns such as the Financial Recession of '08.

Cash Dividends and Stock Dividends are the two major types of dividend payouts. There are other types, but they are not commonly issued by companies:

Property Dividends

Some companies may decide to release non-monetary dividend in lieu of cash or stock dividends.

One example is property dividend, which may either include stocks of a subsidiary company or other physical properties owned by the company such as inventories, equipment, or real estate.

Property dividends are noted at the market value of the distributed asset. You may opt to hold the asset for potential capital gains, but this is often ideal for long-term investment.

Releasing property dividends is usually not a good indicator because this is commonly practiced by companies who don't have enough cash or stocks on hand to issue considerable payouts, or they don't want to liquidate their current shareholdings.

While dividend payouts are regarded as non-cash dividends, they still have a cash value.

Scrip Dividends

Companies who don't have sufficient funds to release dividend payouts anytime soon may choose to issue scrip dividends instead.

Basically, scrip dividends are promissory notes that bind the company to pay shareholders at a specific date.

Scrip dividends are generally payable notes and may or may not involve interest.

Liquidating Dividends

Liquidating dividends is probably not the best type of dividend that you may want to receive because this is often issued by companies who are shutting down.

Once the board of directors of a company votes to close down the business, one of the key decisions they have to make is related to the issuance of liquidating dividends.

The release of liquidating dividends can either be done through a lump-sum payment or several installments.

Publicly listed companies in the US are obligated to issue Form 1099-DIV to all its shareholders. This form contains all the details about the liquidating payouts.

Liquidating dividends have tax advantages for the investor. However, these benefits may not be sufficient to cover initial investment because the original value of the company when you have purchased the stocks might have already drastically decreased.

Advantages of Stock Dividend Investing

Getting dividend payouts is somehow similar to earning interest from your bank deposits. It is nice to receive the fruits of your investment, but other investors are after the thrill of betting on the volatility of the stock prices.

Some stock investors or traders love the thrilling experience particularly when the prices are soaring. But if your risk tolerance is not that high, investing in dividend stocks could balance out the volatility in the stock market.

Here are the benefits you may enjoy when you start investing in dividend stocks:

Mild Risk

The stocks of companies that are regularly issuing dividend payouts are usually less volatile. They also have a lower risk-to-reward ratio. As such, these stocks may experience a mild drop in the stock price during an economic downturn.

Mild volatility may also help in the upward movement of the stock price when the market is starting to recover.

Protection Against Inflation

The number one enemy against earning from any investment is inflation. Even a mild inflation rate can take out huge chunks out of your returns.

For example, even if you earn 10% from your investment, a 3% inflation rate will slash out 3 points from your profits.

Financially savvy individuals often use dividend payouts to offset this loss. Companies, on the other hand, are adapting to the inflation trend by adjusting their prices.

So even if the inflation is soaring, the companies can still earn more money, and so they can pay dividends.

Considerable Returns Even in Bear Markets

Companies who have been paying dividends to their shareholders are still motivated to pay their obligations even during bear markets when the stock prices are flat or following a downward trend.

The dividend payouts can help to offset any loss from a decline in stock prices and there are even instances that the returns are still positive.

You Can Use the Payouts to Buy More Shares

When you buy a specific number of stocks of a non-dividend company, you can only acquire that specific number of stocks. This means that if you want to buy more shares, you have to use your own cash to purchase extra units.

If you buy dividend stocks, you can purchase extra shares by reinvesting in the company. It is unnecessary to use your own cash on hand to purchase more stocks. And if you are enrolled in a reinvestment program, the process will be easier.

Earn Passive Income

Stock dividends can provide you with a regular flow of passive returns, which you can choose to spend or reinvest in the same shares or other instruments.

In fact, this is the primary advantage that entices many stock investors who are looking for investment plus supplemental regular income.

Strong Companies

Only established and strong companies can issue regular dividend payouts. Startups often are not in the best position to pay dividends as they are more motivated to reinvest most of their returns to sustain their growth.

Remember, the company board of directors will only decide to issue dividends if the company has already achieved solid milestones and they believe it can sustain profitability and payouts in the long run.

Moreover, the obligation to issue dividend payouts will compel the company leaders to be more responsible and more cautious in the way they operate the business.

Baby Boomer Demand

Stock market experts believe that the price for dividend stocks can continue to go up as the demand for it will be fired up by the baby boomers who are now in retirement and searching for additional sources of passive income.

Even though this is a carefully studied projection, there's no guarantee that this demand would hold up. Still, the probability of this becoming true is a lot higher.

Two Methods of Profitability

The profits from the dividend stocks may increase if the companies release dividend payouts and if the prices of shares increase.

If your stocks are non-dividends, the only way you can earn returns from them is though price appreciation, which means you have to sell when the price is high and buy when the price is low.

You Can Retain Ownership of the Stocks

One of the most frustrating features of holding non-dividend stocks is that all your revenues are locked in the investment. The only way to get cash from the investment is by selling your shares.

On the other hand, if you own dividend stocks, you can expect regular returns without losing ownership of the stocks.

Disadvantages of Stock Dividend Investing

Even though investing in dividend stocks carries less risk than non-dividend stocks, it also poses some risk, and not always recommended for all kinds of investors.

Apart from the advantages, you should also understand the disadvantages of buying stocks with dividend payouts. With this, you can decide if this type of stock investment is really the right one for you.

Take note that every time you buy an investment through an intermediary firm like a broker or fund manager, you need to read the fine print no matter how long it is. Within the legalese and technical jargon, it all boils down to the non-guarantee of returns.

This means that your stock dividend investment may earn you money, but it is not guaranteed. And you really need to be sure that you want this investment before you sign any dotted line.

Before you buy a single stock for dividend investing, you should be aware of the following risks:

High Dividend Payout

The dividend payout ratio of a company will reflect how much of its profits are used for growth reinvestment, settle its debts, serve as cash reserves in comparison with the amount paid to stock owners.

Determining the percentage of profits that the company can allocate as dividends is usually complicated. Sure, companies want to attract and retain investors through high payouts. But they also need to keep considerable margins to sustain growth and also to sustain its ability to increase dividends at the same time.

More often than not, when the dividend payout ratio of a company becomes too high to sustain, this may compel the business to decrease the payouts or even cancel the dividends permanently.

Taxation

Double taxation is another drawback of investing in dividend stocks. Once you receive your dividends, you have to pay tax because the company that released the payouts from its net profit should pay tax on its annual profits. These profits generate dividend payouts.

Aside from that form of tax, you also need to pay dues again when you receive the payout in the form of personal income. The IRS will consider your dividends as income that you have earned over the course of a specific taxation year.

So essentially, you are being taxed twice as a shareholder of the company and as individual earning dividends.

Policy Changes

The guidelines used by the company to determine the number of dividends as well as potential increases according to estimated profits constitute the dividend policy.

The share price may be affected if the company makes changes to the dividend policy. More often than not, companies have the discretion to decrease the payout rate or cancel their issuance temporarily or permanently.

Take note that according to the clientele effect theory, the stock price is linked to the response of investors to changes in key policies of a company. Therefore, if there are drastic changes in the dividend policy, there are investors who may decide to start trading their shares.

You may lose a source of passive income if a company suddenly decides to cancel the dividend payouts. But there's also the opportunity to gain from the price appreciation of shares as other investors might sell at a lower price.

Generally, investing in stock dividends has fewer risks in comparison with investing in non-dividend stocks. You have to really understand both the advantages and disadvantages before you purchase any shares.

How to Manage Risks in Dividend Investing

Similar to any form of investment, there is always a risk in stock dividend investing. But the risk is always variable and unpredictable. Some factors can increase the risk of this type of investment. Some of these factors are within your control, while some are not.

While it is impossible to completely get rid of the risk, it is still possible to minimize our risk exposure. You can do this by understanding the factors that play behind the sentiment in the stock market.

Savvy investors are skilled in managing risks in stock dividend investing. They are trained in dealing with factors that are within their control.

Human Error

Human error is actually the biggest risk factor in stock dividend investing, which could lead to the following:

- The disconnect between investment goals and investment strategy
- Allowing emotions to control your decision to buy specific stocks
- Giving in to fear and panic in making decisions
- Lack of research and analysis
- Negligence to monitor market conditions

In order to prevent human error, the best way you can do is performing due diligence.

Let's say you need to jump out of a building during a fire. What would you feel if you are not prepared for such a situation? You will certainly feel extreme fear and you will experience panic that could even worsen your situation.

This is similar to stock dividend investing. What would you feel if you believe that the stock market is crashing? You might panic and decide to cash out all your holdings because you are afraid to lose all your money.

Diversify

Never put all your eggs in one basket. This is a piece of classic investment advice, and it is timeless because it is true.

Stay away from the idea of investing all your money in just one company or one industry. You never know what will happen tomorrow, so don't bet all your cash on one player.

As a mere shareholder, you may not have any voting rights or administrative privileges to direct the company. So, you don't have any control over the business management.

Moreover, the company or even the entire industry may go against the investor sentiment. All of these are beyond your control.

One of the few things that you can control is the investment instruments where you pour your money. You can significantly minimize the risk by distributing your investments in various dividend stocks.

We'll explore the importance of diversifying your dividend investments in Chapter 8.

Let Your Mind Reign Over Your Heart

One of the most popular hypotheses about the mechanics behind the stock market is known as the Efficient Market Hypothesis.

According to this hypothesis, investors are reasonable people who have the ability to understand all the available information in the market to make logical decisions to maximize their returns. But most people are not rational or logical.

There are people who purchase stocks according to the advice of their friends or family, and there are instances that they heed the advice of total strangers.

There are shareholders who trade their stocks because of what they have read in the media or because a new company has introduced a product that they think will be the next big thing. They buy shares even without familiarity with the industry, the background of the company, or the people who are managing it.

In order to manage the risks in stock dividend investing, you should stay away from these three primary emotions: Fear, Greed and Love.

Stock investors who have lost a considerable amount of money in the stock market are often vulnerable to fear that impedes them from taking any action.

Instead of taking on some risk with high potential investments, they would rather bet on conservative instruments with minimal rates of return.

On the other hand, some people are just greedy. These are usually the investors who have made a substantial amount of money in the stock market and are still yearning for more.

Some people are susceptible to following the bandwagon, so they pour money into the hottest industries or companies. The market sentiment usually inflates the bubble that will burst any time.

Greedy investors often invest in financial instruments that they really don't understand but blinded by the promised high returns.

Finally, you should avoid being too fascinated with your stock dividend investments. Bear in mind that your investments are inanimate objects that are not capable of loving you back. But it is quite interesting that these investments can hurt your and betray you if you are negligent and naive.

There are investors who admire the company that they are holding stocks with, so they refuse to sell even if the stock price is falling. Savvy stock investors know how to bail out when the share price starts to decline.

You should regularly review your stocks and analyze every investment in your portfolio. If a particular stock is not growing, you may consider selling your shares. You can easily do this because stocks are easy to liquidate.

How Will You Receive Your Dividend Payouts?

For cash dividends, you will usually receive the payout in the form of a check or electronic bank transfer.

For stock dividends, you will usually receive the payout as stock options. You will not receive any check, but just a notice about the increase in your additional shares. You may choose to cash out your shares or retain it if you think the share price will continue to increase.

Investors who are receiving cash dividends are often sent a check after the former dividend date or the date when the stock starts trading without the declared dividend.

Meanwhile, some companies release extra shares that are equivalent to the value of the dividend payout. This method is called dividend reinvestment and usually offered as an option for dividend payment by individual private companies or mutual funds.

Remember, dividend payouts are taxable income regardless of the method that you have received them.

Some companies have Dividend Reinvestment Plans or DRIPS. If you are interested, just add your existing equity holdings with any added funds from dividend payouts. DRIPs can make the process easier compared to receiving the payout in cash and then using it to buy additional shares.

In-house DRIPs are usually free from agency commissions because there is no need to pay for brokerage fees. This feature makes it attractive for beginners as commissions are proportionately bigger for smaller share purchases.

Another benefit of joining a DRIP is that some companies are providing stockholders a choice to purchase more shares in cash at a much lower rate. The price discount can be as high as 10%, aside from the additional benefits of waived brokerage fees.

Hence, you can purchase more shares at a lower price compared to stock investors who purchase stocks in cash via brokers.

We'll discuss more details about DRIPs in Chapter 10.

When Do Companies Release Dividend Payouts?

Companies who decide to issue dividend payouts will notify their shareholders usually via a formal press release. And for easier reference, the announcement will also be documented through major stock quoting services.

After the announcement, the record date will be determined. The record date refers to the specific date that the shareholders will receive the payout. One day after the record date is known as the ex-date. This refers to the specific date that the stock begins trading at "ex-dividend".

You are not qualified for the dividend payout if you buy shares on an ex-date. The payable date is usually 30 days after the record date. During the payable date, the company will transfer the value of the dividends with the Depository Trust Company (DTC).

The DTC will then distribute the dividends to the different brokerage agencies where shareholders are holding their stocks of the company.

After receiving the payouts, the brokerage agencies will deposit the dividends to individual client accounts.

If the investor is enrolled in a DRIP, the brokerage will start processing the reinvestment plan in accordance with the instruction of the stockholders.

Holders of preferred stocks are often given priority for claiming the earnings and assets of the company. These include the claims for dividends. So preferred stockholders will be paid first, then the rest will be distributed to the owners of common shares.

Chapter Takeaways

In this chapter, we have explored the different important aspects that you need to understand before you start investing in dividend stocks such as:

- The types of dividend stocks (cash dividends, stock dividends, property dividends, scrip dividends, and liquidating dividends)

- The main advantages of investing in dividend stocks include mild risk, hedge against inflation, and a high potential for earning passive income

- The main disadvantages of investing in dividend stocks include high dividend payout, taxation, and susceptibility to policy changes

- Human error is the largest risk in stock dividend investing

- One way to manage risk is to diversify your investments

- As a dividend investor, you should be mindful of the ex-dividend date

Probably, you were scratching your head while reading the first chapter of this book because of some terminologies that you have never heard before.

So, before we proceed with the details of stock dividend investing, it is ideal that we first understand the basic terminology that you will surely encounter in your quest to navigate the world of stock dividend investing.

Let's go to the next chapter!

Chapter 2 - Stock Dividend Investing Terminology

"At the end of the day, dividends are not being paid with margins; dividends are paid with earnings per share." - Joe Kaeser

Performing due diligence is an important pre-business activity that can help you well if you are looking at possible investments.

And in order to properly perform due diligence, you need to understand first the different terms and phrases used in stock dividend investing.

So, in this chapter, we will provide you a brief overview of key terminologies that you will surely encounter as you explore the world of stock dividend investing. '

Debt Equity (D/E) Ratio

Also known as the gearing ratio, the D/E ratio refers to a key metric used in stock dividend analysis. It is used to evaluate the financial leverage of a specific company.

You can calculate the D/E ratio by getting the quotient of the company's total liability by the equity of shareholders. You can look for these numbers of the company balance sheet. Here is the formula for calculating the D/E ratio:

$$Debt/Equity\ Ratio\ =\ \frac{Total\ Liabilities}{Total\ Shareholder\ Equity}$$

If you look at the balance sheet of the company, the assets must be equivalent to the total stockholders' equity minus the liabilities. The categories in the balance sheet may record individual accounts that are commonly considered as debt or equity in the traditional form.

Remember, the ratio can be affected by retained earnings or losses, intangible assets, and pension plan changes. So, a more comprehensive due diligence is needed so you can completely understand the actual leverage of the company.

However, there are instances when the accounts in the primary balance sheet categories are not clear, so there might be a need to change the D/E ratio so your analysis can be more viable and easier to compare between various assets.

You may also improve your evaluation of the D/E ratio by adding short-term leverage ratios, profit performance, and growth expectations.

Due to the fact that the D/E ratio is used to assess the debt of the company relative to the net value of its net assets, this is commonly used to measure the extent to which the business is taking on loans as a method of using its assets as leverage.

The high D/E ratio signifies high risk because it means the company is aggressive in using loans to finance its expansion or growth.

For example, let's say you are comparing the D/E ratio of Company N and Company O with the following details:

Company A

Total shareholder equity: $31.9 million

Total liabilities: $43.54 million

D/E ratio: 1.36

Company B

Total shareholder equity: $8.80 million

Total liabilities: $13.2 million

D/E ratio: 1.50

In a quick analysis, it appears that the high D/E ratio of Company B indicates a higher risk. However, this conclusion is not enough, and you need to perform more due diligence. If Company B is using loans to fund its expansion, it has the potential to earn more revenue than it would have without the loans.

If the loan can increase the revenue by a higher amount in comparison to the cost of debt (interest), then the shareholders will benefit. But if the interest is higher than the revenue generated the share price may plummet. Take note that the loan interests vary according to market conditions, so unprofitable loans may not be significant at the onset.

Changes in assets and long-term loans have the tendency to have the biggest impact on the D/E ratio because these are commonly larger accounts compared to short-term debt and assets.

It is ideal to use other metrics and ratios if you want to analyze the short-term debt of the company against its capacity to pay the loan for the year.

For example, if you want to compare the solvency or short-term liquidity, you may use the cash ratio (short term liabilities + cash and marketable securities) or the present ratio (short term assets + short term liabilities) instead of the long-term metrics for leverage like D/E ratio.

It is important to take a closer look into the industry of the company you are analyzing if you want to use D/E ratio. Because different sectors have different growth rates and capital requirements, a high D/E ratio might be typical in one industry, while a low ratio might be the norm in another industry.

For example, tech companies commonly have D/E ratio lower than 0.5 while capital intensive industries like manufacturing have D/E ratio beyond 2.

Companies in the utility sector usually have a very high ratio as against market averages. Utilities have a slower growth rate but have the capacity to sustain a constant income stream, which allows the companies to borrow at a lower interest rate.

High D/E ratios in slow-growth industries that have stable revenue indicate capital efficiency. The non-cyclical consumer industries tend to also have D/E ratio because these companies have stable revenue and may borrow money at a much lower interest rate.

But take note that preferred shares are usually considered as equity while the liquidation right, preferred dividends and par value make the form of equity appear like debt.

Adding preferred shares in total debt may boost the D/E ratio and make the company less enticing for investment. Adding preferred shares in the equity part of the ratio may lower the ratio and increase the denominator. This can be a major concern for companies like REITs wherein the preferred shares are added in the D/E ratio.

Dividend Coverage Ratio (DCR)

DCR is a key metric in stock dividend investing, which will allow you to measure the number of times that a certain company is releasing dividends to its stockholders.

You can calculate the dividend coverage ratio by getting the quotient of the net income by the number of dividends issued to the shareholders.

The net profit refers to the earnings of the company after paying all expenses including all taxes payable. As you already know, dividend payout refers to the number of dividends released to shareholders.

But there are several types of DCR that you might encounter when you analyze the figures of stock dividends.

The first type of DCR is often used to determine the number of times that a company may issue dividends to common shareholders if the company also has preferred shareholders to consider.

Here is the formula for this type of DCR:

(Net Profit - Required Preferred Dividend Payouts) / Number of Dividends Released to Common Stockholders

This type can also be used to determine the number of times that a company is capable of releasing dividends to preferred shareholders. Here is the formula:

Net Profit / Dividends Released to Preferred Stockholders

When the DCR is higher than 1, it means that the revenue generated by the company is enough to issue dividends to shareholders.

On the other hand, a consistently low DCR often signifies that the company may lose profits in the foreseeable future because it is not capable of sustaining its current level of dividend payouts.

Although the DCR is a good indicator to determine the risk for choosing stock dividends, there are important concerns with this key metric that you must consider.

First, you should remember that the DCR doesn't represent the actual cash flow. In calculating the DCR of a company, you can use the net profit in the numerator. So, a company may report high net income but don't have the actual cash for dividend payouts.

Another point of concern is that the DCR is not a reliable metric to use to analyze the future risk. Remember, the net income changes every fiscal year. Therefore, getting a high DCR according to the record of the company's performance is not always a valid indicator of dividend risk.

Nonetheless, the DCR is still typically used by stock analysts and investors to estimate the risk level that is related to receiving the dividends from the stock investment.

Dividend Growth Rate

The Dividend Growth Rate refers to the annual growth (expressed in percentage) that a particular stock dividend experiences over a particular duration.

This key metric is important for using the dividend discount model that is a form of security pricing model. It works under the assumption that the projected dividends will affect the price of a specific stock without considering the excess of company growth over the projected dividend growth of the stock.

In using the dividend discount model, a specific stock could be perceived as undervalued if the result is higher as opposed to the existing price of the company shares. Projecting the expected value of revenue flow using this model can help you calculate the intrinsic value of a specific stock.

A track record of stable dividend growth may indicate dividend growth that also signifies profitability for a particular company. If you need to determine the dividend growth rate, you may use any interval time that you prefer. You can also calculate the dividend growth rate by analyzing the annual figure over a certain period.

By using the linear method, you can take the average dividend growth rate. For example, let's say that Company C issued the following dividend payouts to its shareholders over the last five years:

2015 = $1.00

2016 = $1.05

2017 = $1.07

2018 = $1.11

2019 = $1.15

To calculate the growth rate from 2015 to 2018, you can use this formula:

Year X Dividend / (Year X - 1 Dividend)

- A

By using that formula, we have determined the following growth rates within five years:

2015 = N/A

2016 = $1.05 / $1.00 - 1 = 5%

2017 = $1.07 / $1.05 - 1 = 1.9%

2018 = $1.11 / $1.07 - 1 = 3.74%

2019 = $1.15 / $1.11 - 1 = 3.6%

The average annual growth for Company C is 35.6%

To determine the value of the Company C stocks, you can use the dividend discount model, which is based on the idea that a stock will be the sum of the future payments to shareholders that is discounted back to the present date.

The formula for the dividend discount model is $P = D_1 / (r-g)$, which has three key variables to obtain the existing price:

D_1 = dividend value for next year

r = capital cost equity

g = dividend growth rate

In our example, if the dividend for 2020 will be at $1.18, and the capital cost equity is 8%, the stock price for each share is estimated to hit $26.58.

Dividend Payout Ratio

Dividend Payout Ratio is the percentage of profits released by a company to its stockholders. This is often written as a percentage, but there are instances that you will encounter this ratio as cash flow proportion.

To calculate the Dividend Payout Ratio, the following formulae are used:

(Dividends Per Share (DPS) / Earnings Per Share (EPS)) x 100

or

(Total Paid Dividends / Net Income) x 100

Companies usually release dividend payouts at the end of the fiscal year. The dividends come from the net profits of the company and will be considered as returns to stockholders.

The DPR is a key financial metric used to determine the sustainability of the company's dividend payouts. This corresponds to the number of dividends released by the company in accordance with its total net profit.

For example, Company D has profits per share of $4 and the dividend payout ratio of 80 percent. Company E has profits per share of $4 and the dividends for every share of the dollar has 50 %.

So, if you are the investor, which stocks will you choose? Company D or Company E?

Actually, the data is not enough in this example, because you need to know the sector of these companies before you invest. There's no single metric that can figure out if a payout ratio is good.

Companies in defensive sectors such as utilities, pipelines, and telecommunications have stable and predictable revenue and can support higher dividend payouts.

Companies in cyclical sectors such as energy have unstable and difficult to predict revenue flow, and so it cannot promise higher payouts as opposed to defensive companies.

In our example above, if Company D is a producer of commodities, and Company E is a regulated company, the payout sustainability of Company D seems to be better if you compare it with Company D despite the fact that Company E has a lower payout ratio.

Some companies issue all their profits to stockholders while some companies only release a specific portion of their revenue. If a company is paying out some of the revenue like dividends, then it will keep the rest of the profits.

Plowback Ratio (we will discuss this in a bit) is used to measure the profits retained by the business.

If the business is using more of its profits for operation or growth, then the payout ratio will be lower, and the retention ratio is higher.

If the business is sharing more of its profits with its stockholders, then the payout ratio is higher, and the retention ratio is lower.

If the payout ratio exceeds 100%, it means that the business is paying out more dividends compared to its profits. While this may appear attractive for investors, this move is considered as bad practice.

Stock dividend companies that are releasing payouts regularly have a target range for their dividend payout ratios and identify them as sustainable earnings or cash flow.

A stable payout ratio of a company signifies that the business has a strong record of dividend payouts.

Despite their increases in dividend payouts, blue-chip companies have stable payout ratios.

Dividend Yield

Dividend Yield refers to the ratio of the annual dividend of the business as opposed to its stock price. This is written as a percentage and could be calculated using the formula below:

Yearly Dividend / Share Price

The annual dividend used in the formula could be the most recent dividend x 4, the total dividends released by the company during the last fiscal year, or the total dividend paid over the past four quarters.

The dividend yield also signifies the dividend-only ROI. This yield will decrease when the price of the shares increases, and it will increase if the price of the shares declines if the dividend is not increased or decreased.

The yield often looks high for stocks that are quickly declining because the yield responds to the price fluctuation.

Consider the following examples:

- Company F has a current share price of $40 and an annual dividend of $1 for each share
- Company G has a current share price of $80 and an annual dividend of $1 for each share.

Using the above formula, the dividend yield of Company F is at 2.5% (1/40 = 0.025) and the dividend yield of Company G is only 1.25% (1/80).

Considering other factors are stable, the better stock to buy is Company F because it has a double dividend yield compared to Company G.

While high dividend yields appear attractive, it can affect the cost of the potential growth of the company. Remember, the money that the company is paying as dividends to shareholders is the money that it cannot use for expansion or generate capital gains. Shareholders can expect more returns if the share price increases while they are still the owners of the company.

Based on historical data, a concentration on dividends may boost profits. Since 1960, around 82 % of the total profits of S&P companies are being derived from dividends (Hartford Funds). This has been validated several times because it operates under the assumption that investors are attracted to reinvest their dividends back to the business. This considerably strengthens the capacity of the business and the shareholders to earn more money in the long run.

Established businesses that are no longer aggressive in their expansion are paying the highest dividend yields. Companies in the staples or utilities sectors are ideal examples of sectors that are paying the best dividend yield.

Meanwhile, the dividend yield is virtually lower in tech companies. However, the rule about established companies also applies to this sector.

Bear in mind that the dividend yield cannot be used to tell you much about what type of dividend that a company is paying.

For example, the dividend yield in the market is considered the highest for Real Estate Investment Trusts (REITs).

However, these are mostly derived from dividends that are quite different than conventionally qualified dividends.

Master Limited Partnerships (MLP) and Business Development Companies (BDC) have high average dividend yields. These types of businesses are mandated by the government to share their profits with stockholders.

Take note that it is not ideal to use the dividend yield to assess the stock because dividend data might be based on erroneous data or are already obsolete. Many companies have a high yield as their stock falls. This often happens before canceling the dividend payout.

Instead, you may use the updated financial report of a company to calculate its dividend yield. But this is ideal to do during Q1 after the company has released its annual financial report.

But if you are already on Q2, Q3, and Q4, the information will no longer be reliable. As a workaround, you can obtain the total of the last four quarters of dividends that may cover the trailing year of data. But take note that this data may not be enough if there are significant changes in the dividend payouts.

Companies are usually releasing dividend payouts every quarter. Hence, investors are looking at the last quarterly dividend, then they multiply it by 4 and use the result as the annual dividend. This may help you assess the recent changes in the payouts. This method only works if the company is paying a dividend every quarter.

Some companies are paying a minimum dividend every quarter, then a higher dividend at the end of the year. So, you may obtain a bloated dividend yield if you calculate the figure after the release of the annual dividend.

Although rare, there are companies who are releasing payouts monthly. So, using the figure for a monthly payout may result in lower dividend yield.

To determine the best way to calculate the dividend yield, you must look at the historical data of dividend payouts, so you can select the most suitable method that will provide you the best results.

You must also be careful in evaluating a company with a higher dividend yield. Take note that the share price is the denominator in the equation. Therefore, a sudden decline in the price may considerably inflate the result.

Ex-Dividend Date

Ex-Dividend Date refers to the day that the stock starts trading without the value of the current dividend payout.

If you purchase shares on or after the ex-dividend date, you will not be entitled to the announced dividend. If you purchase a share before the ex-dividend date, you will be eligible to receive the payout.

The price of the stock usually declines in price by the value of the expected payout because investors are not eligible for the next payout on the ex-dividend date.

When the company decides to release a dividend payout, the board of directors will figure out a record date. Be mindful of the record date because this is when you must be included in the list of shareholders so you can be eligible for the dividend payout.

After identifying the record date, the ex-dividend date is also set according to the rules of the stock exchange in which the stock will be traded. Therefore, the ex-dividend date is often one business day before the record date.

For example, if a company announced a dividend on July 3 with a record date on Monday, August 11, the ex-dividend date will be August 8 because this is one business day before the ex-dividend date.

It is important to remember that the ex-dividend date occurs prior to the record date because of the way stock trades are settled. During the trade, the transaction will be recorded after two business days, which is known as the T+2 payment.

Therefore, if you purchase the shares on August 14 but you have sold the stocks on August 15, you are still considered a stock owner of the company because the record will show the incomplete trade. If you sell your shares on August 14, then the trade will be settled on August 18 and the new holder of the shares will be eligible for the dividend payout.

But what if the company issues dividends in the form of stocks instead of cash? There are slight differences in this case. With stock dividends, the ex-dividend date will be documented on the first business day when the dividends are settled.

For example, let's say that Company H announced in a press release dated October 5, 2017, that it will begin trading ex-dividend on October 5 and the record date was identified as October 6.

Before the announcement, Company H already confirmed that the dividend payout of 0.72 per share is scheduled for November 2. Hence, shareholders who purchased the stocks from the company prior to the ex-date of October 5 will be eligible for the payout.

Why is it important for investors to really understand the ex-dividend date? You have to buy dividend stocks at least two days before the record date because it will take two days to pay the trade.

Understanding this mechanism can help you plan out your trade, especially if your strategy for investment is concentrated on income. But because the price of the shares usually declines by around the equivalent amount of the payout, buying shares prior to the ex-dividend payout will unlikely provide you any revenue. In the same vein, investors buying stocks on the ex-dividend date or after may take advantage of a lower stock price.

There is a tendency for the stock price to drop by a certain percentage during the payout. This movement in price is triggered by small dividends and not easy to detect even by those who have been trading in stock dividends for years. It is a lot easier to keep track of the stock price fluctuation during huge dividend payouts.

Aside from the ex-dividend date, there are other important dates that you should take note:

Announcement Date

Also referred to as the declaration date, the announcement date refers to the specific date that the company declares the dividend payout. This is a crucial date to remember because any change in the payout may cause the price of the stocks to fluctuate as traders are still observing the market.

Record Date

Record date refers to the specific date that the company will review its list of stockholders. The record date is often a day after the ex-dividend date. Although important to note, the record date is not the main factor that should influence your investments in stock dividends.

Payment Date

Payment Date refers to the specific date when dividend payouts are released either through checks or electronic transfers. This event usually doesn't have any effect on the stock price because the payment data is already announced before the payment date.

Plowback Ratio

Plowback Ratio (also known as Retention Ratio) refers to the portion of the revenue that is plowbacked or retained by the business. This portion is known as the retained revenue.

The business may decide to retain the profits to acquire new assets, begin new projects, or expand business operations.

Plowback Ratio is the opposite of the Payout Ratio that is used to measure the percentage of profits released to shareholders as dividends.

The formula below is used to calculate the retention ratio of the business:

(Net Income - Dividends) / Net Income

Price-Earnings Ratio (P/E Ratio)

P/E Ratio is often used to value a company by measuring its current share price in relation to its per-share revenue. Some stock traders call this price multiple or earnings multiple.

Here is the formula used to determine the P/E ratio of a company:

Market Value per Share / Earnings per Share

Basically, the P/E ratio signifies the dollar value that a stockholder can expect to invest in the business so it can receive a certain amount of profit from the company. This is the main reason why this figure is also known as price multiple. By looking at the P/E ratio, it will show you how much traders are willing to pay to earn dividends from the stocks.

Let's say Company I is currently trading at a multiple of 20. This signifies that an investor is willing to pay $20 for every dollar of the current profits.

To determine the P/E ratio, the Earnings Per Share (EPS) should be given, which is often derived by analyzing the company figures from the recent four quarters.

This form of P/E ratio is known as the trailing P/E, which can be computed by searching for the difference between the share value of the company at the start of the year.

There are also cases that the P/E can be derived by estimating the profits projected for the next four quarters. This form of P/E is known as a projected or forward P/E. Other stock analysts are using other types of P/E which use the sum of the numbers from the last two quarters and estimate for the next two quarters.

A high P/E ratio signifies that investors are expecting high revenue growth in the future as opposed to companies with low P/E. Meanwhile, low P/E may indicate that a company is currently undervalued or that the company is just doing well in comparison to its historical trends.

When a company is reporting losses, P/E will appear as N/A. While it is not impossible to get negative P/E, it is not common in stock trading.

P/E ratio is also known as a method to standardize the value of dollar profits in the stock market. In theory, you can obtain the median of P/E ratios over a specific period so you can determine the standard P/E ratio. Stock analysts often use this as a benchmark to figure out if a specific stock is good to buy or not.

Like other fundamental signals used to determine the stocks to buy, P/E ratio also has its limitations. P/E ratio is just one metric to look at and always remember that there is no single metric that can absolutely help you choose the stocks that will win each time.

One primary restriction of using P/E ratio dwells in comparing the ratios of various companies. Valuations as well as growth rates of companies often vary between sectors because of the different methods that businesses are generating revenue. Moreover, companies have different timelines for earning money.

It is ideal to use P/E ratio if you are comparing companies in the same sector as the insights you can obtain will be highly reliable. You can't say that your assumptions are valid if you compare the ratio of an internet company versus an energy company.

So be sure to use P/E ratios of different companies but are within the same sector. For example, a telecom company might have a high P/E ratio, but this could signify a trend in the sector and not the company itself. If the whole sector has a high P/E ratio, the high ratio of the company you are eyeing is not that valuable.

Moreover, leverage can also impact P/E ratios because the debt of a company may affect both the profits as well as the prices of the same sector. They will have different takes on their accounts payable.

Company J has a lower debt and has a lower P/E ratio compared to Company K who has higher payables. But if the sector is doing great, Company J has the higher potential to earn more because of its decision to take some high yield risks.

The equation in calculating the P/E ratio also causes one major limitation. Accurate inputs of the market value of shares can affect the accurate and objective presentations of P/E ratio as well as accurate profits for share estimates.

While the stock market defines the share value, this is quite unlikely to be applied for profits that are commonly reported by companies. So, these figures are not totally reliable. Changing the profit report can also change the P/E ratio because revenue is a key variable for calculating P/E ratio.

Return on Equity (ROE)

Return on Equity (ROE) is a key metric used to assess the financial performance of a company. You can calculate the ROE by getting the quotient of the shareholder's equity and net profit.

This is also known as the return on net assets because the equity of stockholders is equivalent to the assets of the company minus the loan payables.

ROE is expressed as a percentage and could be determined if the net income and equity are both positive. Net income is calculated before the payout for common shares and after the payout for preferred shares.

The level of ROE will significantly vary from one industry to another. The comparison will be more accurate if you use this metric to evaluate companies in the same industry.

However, there are instances that your assessment could be misleading if you compare the ROE of a company that is paying high dividends versus a company that is paying low dividends.

The workaround for this is to analyze the net income of the company over the latest fiscal year or also known as the trailing income. This will provide you with a more accurate insight into the financial activity of the company over the last 12 months.

You should also look at the balance sheet of the company to look at the shareholder's equity. This balance sheet refers to the running balance of the company's whole record of changes in assets and liabilities. It is best to calculate ROE according to the average equity over 12 months because of the differences between the balance sheet and income statement.

$$ROE = \frac{Net\ Income}{Average\ Shareholder\ Equity}$$

You can determine the average shareholder equity by adding the equity at the beginning of the period to the equity at the end of the period. Then divide the number by 2. You can use the quarterly balance sheets to guide you in finding the equity average.

For example, Company L has an annual income of $250 million. The average equity of stockholders stands at $800 million. The ROE of this company would be at 31.25%.

Remember, you should avoid comparing the ROE of two companies from different sectors. Some investors consider ROE near the long-term average of 10 to 20% as an ideal ratio. Anything that hits below 10% is considered poor ROE.

ROE is ideal to use to project the future estimates of the growth rate of shares and the growth rate of the stock dividends. These two calculations can be used to compare company stocks from the same industry.

In order to obtain the future growth rate of a company, you can multiply the ROE by the retention ratio, which refers to the portion of net profit retained by the company to boost its growth.

For example, Company M and Company N both have the same ROE and net income, but they have different retention ratios. The ROE of Company M is 15 % and its profits are at 30 %, which indicates that it is retaining 70 % of its net revenue.

Meanwhile, Company N also has an ROE of 15 % but only pays 10 % of its revenue to its stockholders. This indicates that this company is retaining 90% of its revenue for expansion, growth, acquisition, or other purposes.

The growth rate of Company M is 10.5% because

15% (ROE) X 70% (Retention Ratio) = 10.5%

The growth rate of Company N is 13.5% because

15% (ROE) X 90% (Retention Ratio) = 13.5 %

This calculation follows the sustainable growth model that can be used to predict the future of a particular company and determine which stocks to buy. But this can be risky because you might go over the sustainable range for growth capacity.

Companies with a low growth rate, as opposed to its sustainable rate, could be undervalued or the market fails to notice the red flags. The growth rate that is above or below the sustainable rate needs intensive due diligence.

With the earlier assessment, Company M appears more attractive than Company N. But this overlooks the advantages of a higher dividend rate that can entice investors. You may adjust the computation to estimate the dividend growth rate of the stock, which is more important for stock dividend investors.

You can determine the estimated dividend growth rate by multiplying the ROE by payout ratio, which refers to the percentage of net profit that is paid to common shareholders through dividends. This method can provide you a more sustainable dividend growth that makes Company N more attractive.

The growth rate of Company N is 4.5 % because 15% (ROE) x 30% (Payout Ratio) = 4.5%

The growth rate of Company M is only 1.5% because 15% (ROE) X 10% (Payout Ratio) = 1.5%

Companies with growth rates beyond the sustainable rate may signify some red flags, so be sure to perform due diligence first before you buy their stocks.

How to Use ROE for Comparing Stocks

The value of ROE for stock analysis will largely depend on looking at the stocks relative to its category. For example, if you look at the balance sheet of a utility company, you may find big assets and debt account. The usual ROE for companies in the utility sector is 10% or lower.

Meanwhile, retail companies usually have smaller balance sheet accounts, but their ROE can hit as high as 18 % or even higher.

As a benchmark, you may target companies with ROE that is equivalent or just a bit higher than the average for the industry.

For example, let's say that Company O has maintained its ROE at 18% over five years as opposed to other companies in the same sector that can only hit 15% at most. This indicates that the management of the company has gone beyond utilizing its assets for income generation.

More often than not, high ROE is a good indicator, especially if the net profit is extremely big as opposed to company equity because the company's performance could be strong. However, high ROE can be caused by a small equity account as opposed to net profit, which signifies risk.

If a company has a negative profit, the ROE is not calculated. But you may sometimes see negative ROE because of excessive loans, long-term pattern of share buybacks, or a period of losses. This results in negative ROE.

The usual concern with negative ROE is excessive loans or unstable revenue streams. However, this rule is not absolute as there are profitable companies who are using their revenue to buy their own shares. So be very careful in interpreting the ROE.

For some companies, this is an alternative way of issuing dividends and it may reduce the equity that is enough to cause negative ROE. You must study this further if you are dealing with stock dividends that have unusually high or negative ROE. In some instances, the negative ROE could be caused by a buyback scheme using the company profits.

Bear in mind that you should not compare companies with negative ROE against companies with positive ROE. The results will not be reliable.

How about companies that are not making money? Let's say that you are analyzing the stocks of Company P that is not making significant profits for three years. The losses are added in the balance sheet and labeled as a retained loss.

The losses will decrease the stockholder equity and will be presented as a negative value. But recently, the company launched a new product that significantly increased its profitability.

After the product launch and record sales, the denominator in the ROE formula will be quite small considering the business has been bleeding money for the past three years. This results in the company's ROE to be high and unreliable.

For experienced stock investors, the high ROE of Company P indicates that it has minimal profitability in the past three to four years. Buying shares from this company poses a lot of risk as opposed to buying stocks of companies with lower ROE and stable profit margins.

Meanwhile, companies that are on a loan spree may record high ROE because equity is equivalent to the assets minus debt. The surge in the loans payable could lead to lower equity.

A common scenario for this to happen is if the company is taking huge loans to buy its own shares. This can increase the earnings per share of the company, but it will not affect its actual growth rates.

Analyzing the ROE of different companies can help you choose stock dividends, but you must be cautious in comparing companies who are not in the same sector and who have different strategies in issuing dividend payouts.

Chapter Takeaways

In this chapter, we have learned the most important terms in stock dividend investing:

- Debt Equity (D/E) Ratio

- Dividend Coverage Ratio (DCR)

- Dividend Growth Rate

- Dividend Payout Ratio

- Dividend Yield

- Ex-Dividend Date

- Plowback Ratio

- Price-Earnings Ratio (P/E) Ratio

- Return on Equity (ROE)

Understanding the different terms used in stock dividend investing will arm you with the knowledge to better make sense of this investment strategy.

It will be easier for you to choose the stock dividends with more chances to provide you with a regular income if you know these terms, and what they mean in the stock market.

Now that you are familiar with the key metrics used in stock dividends, it is time to get to know the different factors you need to consider before you choose dividend stocks.

Chapter 3 - Six Important Factors to Consider Before Buying Stock Dividends

"Do you know the only thing that gives me pleasure? It's to see my dividends coming in." - John D. Rockefeller

Before you buy stocks from companies that are paying dividends, you need to consider the following factors:

1. Dividend Yield

2. Profit Growth Rate

3. Balance Sheet

4. Debt Volume

5. Sales Performance

6. Prevailing Tax Laws for Dividend Investments

In this chapter, we will explore each factor, then discuss particular circumstances, which you can use to help you choose stock dividends.

Dividend Yield

Releasing dividend payouts is one indicator that the company's finances are in order. As you already know, the

Dividend Yield refers to the ratio that indicates the dividend income for each share divided by the price for every share.

For instance, a stock that is priced at $50 each and pays $5 dividend has a 2.5% dividend yield.

If you're looking for stocks for long-term dividend investment, Dividend Yield is a key metric that you must first look into. You can use the dividends to buy more shares, so you don't have to use your own money to grow your stock holdings.

Some stock investors depend on dividend yields for their passive income. Even though the income from dividends is not as guaranteed as fixed-income instruments such as bonds, most dividends generate valuable income in the long run.

But savvy investors do not only assess Dividend Yield as this short-term analysis can be misleading. Some companies choose to continue issuing dividends even if their profits are low. Meanwhile, there are also companies that are paying high dividends so they cannot reinvest for their growth.

It is ideal to compare the Dividend Yield with the Total Profits of the company. The latter is a direct representation of how much the investment has actually generated for the shareholder.

The Dividend Yield will provide you an insight into the actual cash dividend. Meanwhile, the Total Profit will involve the interest as well as the share price increases alongside dividend and other capital gains.

At first glance, Total Profits seem to provide a more encompassing and useful metric to assess the performance of the stocks as opposed to the Dividend Yield. However, the Total Profits are totally retrospective of the share prices that may increase for different reasons. It is usually more difficult to estimate the performance of the future investment from the profits of shares in comparison with Dividend Yield.

Selecting between the Total Profits and the Dividend Yield in evaluating your potential stock investments could be tricky.

Total Profits is a more helpful metric to consider if you have to determine the stocks that have performed better within a specific duration. Meanwhile, analyzing the Dividend Yield of a company is more useful if you are interested to invest in stocks that will provide you with a regular income.

It is more reasonable to concentrate on the Total Profits if you have a long-term investment strategy and you are more interested to keep your stock equities for several years.

Also, bear in mind that you should not only limit your analysis in these two metrics if you want to assess a company for possible equity investment. Rather, you must carefully look at the balance sheet and the income statement and always perform due diligence.

Relative Dividend Yield Strategy

The Relative Dividend Strategy is often used by stock investors to compare the yield of a particular stock to the yield of an entire sector. With this, you can determine if a stock is underpriced or overvalued.

RDY is a long-term strategy, which can provide you with considerable revenue after a minimum of three years. So, this is not recommended for those who are looking for quick returns.

Furthermore, this approach doesn't rely on P/E ratio, past earnings, or projected revenue to calculate the valuations. This strategy will encourage you to be more patient, disciplined, and self-reliant, which will empower you to focus on big companies who are struggling with the current market condition, but are already established organizations that are well-positioned for fast recovery.

Using absolute yield to identify undervalued stocks in the market can help you narrow down mature companies in slow-growth industries.

Stock investors who are using the RDY strategy are often looking for capital appreciation. Remember, the yield in this strategy doesn't require to be high but just a bit higher compared to the market price. Therefore, this strategy can help you identify potential investment opportunities in both weak and strong markets.

In the long run, RDY can help you build an investment portfolio with a higher stream of income, which is around 2 % higher than the S&P index.

RDY can also help you understand the current investor sentiment. A low RDY signifies the general enthusiasm of investors while high RDY signifies general distress in the market.

If you are skilled in using this strategy, it will be easy for you to sell stock dividends even if other investors are buying or buy stocks even if the majority of the investors are selling.

Take note that the stocks that you have identified by using RDY have the tendency to have a lower risk compared to the rest of the stocks in the dividends market because they are often not eyed by most investors.

In using RDY, you can identify potential stocks that are already underperforming in the market for a while. Hence, there is a lower chance that the share price will further decline because it has already surpassed the lowest peak.

The stocks that you have identified through RDY tend to have higher average yields. Stock investors who are using this strategy are skilled not to buy stocks until the yield is typically at least 50 % higher than the market average.

Therefore, in using RDY, it will be easier for you to determine the stocks that are undervalued and are expected to eventually see capital gains when it comes to the share price. Still, the high level of yield is more likely to signify a considerable value for investor returns.

You should also take note that in holding equities for an extended duration, you will be allowed to sell around 25% to 30% of your portfolio in a certain year. This can be lower as opposed to an almost 100% turnover rate in most mutual funds.

However, low turnover could result in lower transaction fees that will provide you with more cash for reinvestment and for the generation of higher revenue. Lower sales can also mean lower capital gains and tax bills.

The recommended holding period for dividend stocks that you have identified through RDY is at least three years. When the share prices of these stocks start to recover, it can lead to the relative yield of the stock to decline below the market yield that could trigger a sell signal.

Investment portfolios under RDY typically contain established corporations that have a consistent record of paying dividends. These stocks have lower volatility in comparison to the general market during bear markets.

The RDY Strategy can provide you with the signals when to buy and sell according to the yield. However, this investment strategy may seem a bit more complex in comparison with the dividend connection that utilizes absolute yield.

Profit Growth Rate

The company's profit growth rate is another factor that you must analyze to determine if its stocks are worth buying. Analyzing the profit growth rate will let you gain insights into the potential dividend increase of a company.

In choosing stocks for your dividend investment portfolio, one of the first metrics that you should take a closer look at is the company's earnings.

Carefully look at the record of earnings of the company. What is the trend? Is it growing? Stagnant? Or Declining?

It is fairly hard for a company to sustain growth if its revenues are not increasing. You must search for stocks of companies with an outstanding reputation for increasing the amount of cash they generate through sales.

Apart from the amount of revenue, the next metric that you should look into is the net profit, which refers to the money that the company retains after it has paid all its dues such as taxes, wages, and other payables.

The profits of the company are influenced by various factors like operational expenses, liabilities, financing, and assets. To detect if there's a pattern for consistent growth, you should look into Earnings Per Share (EPS) of the company stocks.

EPS refers to the percentage of the profits that are reserved for each share of the common stocks. Analyzing this number will tell you if the company is profitable or not.

To determine the EPS of a company, you have to look first for the weighted average number of common stocks, net profit, then dividend payouts released for holders of preferred stocks. All these figures can be found in the balance sheet and income statement of a company.

In determining the EPS, it is ideal to use the weighted average number of common shares instead of the reporting term. This is due to the fact that the number of shares is always changing. Moreover, any stock dividends or splits must be included in the calculation of the weighted average of outstanding stocks.

The capital required to generate net profits is an important figure in determining EPS. However, many stock investors ignore this, which is not a good practice. Two corporations may present the same EPS, but they might have different net assets. Choose stocks from a company that demonstrates efficiency in using its capital to generate more income.

While the EPS is commonly used to keep track of the performance of a company, stockholders usually don't have access to it. A portion of the earnings could be issued in the form of dividend, but a higher percentage of the EPS will be retained by the company.

To receive more EPS, a shareholder may appeal to their representatives to modify the percentage of EPS reserves for dividends. Because shareholders don't have access to the EPS, the connection between the EPS and share price might be difficult to identify. This is usually true for companies that are not paying dividends.

Before the board of directors of a company decides to implement a cycle of increasing dividend payouts, it should consider sustainability. The management will be responsible for increasing the revenue to make sure that the cash flow every year will be enough to pay dividends and retain enough profits for growth.

If the revenue is not following an upward trend, then the company may be compelled to decrease, suspend, or cancel the dividend payouts. This will usually lead to a significant price fall of the stocks.

Business executives are often under pressure to do everything to prevent any price fall because they are also compensated in stock options on top of cash.

The track record of the company in growing its dividend is a strong sign that a company has the ability to grow its dividends in the next few years. Another strong signal that supports this insight is a low payout ratio.

Balance Sheet

In determining the viability of the stock investment, expert stock traders usually start by looking into the balance sheet of a company. This will provide you with an overview of the assets and liabilities of a company in a specific period of time.

Crunching numbers is an important activity for stock investors. Most stock investors look into the top line or the cash that is considered as the most important figure in the balance sheet.

You must also look into the company properties, short-term investments, accounts receivable, and other receivables. The three major categories found in a balance sheet are 1) assets, 2) liabilities, and 3) equity.

All company assets should be identified either as current or non-current. Assets are categorized as current if they can be converted to cash within 1 year. Cash, net receivables, and inventories are all significant current assets because they are flexible and easy to liquidate.

Cash is located at the top of the balance sheet. Corporations that are generating huge amounts of cash are often performing well in delivering their products and services, and collecting payments.

You should look further into the company figures if the topline is too high or too low. But remember, there are companies that don't need to require a huge volume of cash for its operations. Rather, they choose to reinvest the extra cash into the business to enhance its operations. Some businesses also increase their dividend payouts if there is extra cash.

Like assets, liabilities are also identified as current or non-current. Current liabilities are the accounts payable of the company that should be paid within the year. Companies with minimal liabilities are ideal for stock investments, especially if you compare it to the cash flow of the company. Avoid stocks of companies who have a lot of debt.

Common liabilities include accounts payable, long-term loans, customer deposits, and deferred profits. Although assets are often tangible and immediate, liabilities, on the other hand, are considered as equally important. This is because debts and other liabilities must be paid before spending the profit.

Finally, the third important figure that you should look into in a company's balance sheet is equity. This one refers to the assets minus the liabilities, and represents how much the stockholders of a company actually own. In evaluating stocks, you should take a closer look at the retained profits as well as paid-in capital that you can usually find in the equity section.

Paid-in capital signifies the initial amount invested by stockholders for their shares. You have to compare this to the additional paid-in capital to obtain the equity that premium investors paid higher than the par value.

During mergers and acquisitions, many investors or funding groups will always look into equity.

Retained profits will allow you to see the amount of profit that the company is using to pay its debt rather than distributing to stockholders in the form of dividend payouts.

Most of the details you need to evaluate the company's debt can be obtained from the balance sheet.

However, not all debt obligations and assets are recorded in the balance sheet. Some companies own intangible assets the actual value of which can be difficult to determine. These include patents, trademarks, copyrights, and business processes. These are all considered assets today, but they are not recorded in the company's balance sheet.

Debt Volume

It is crucial to study different financial records of a company before you buy its stocks. Among the most important financial metrics that you should assess is the debt volume of the company.

Stock investors are looking into the company's debt to check if it will affect the dividend investment. But first, we need to study the various forms of loans that companies usually have.

Companies often borrow money using two main methods:

1. Securing loans from banks or other credit organizations

2. Issuance of fixed-income debt instruments like bonds, notes, or bills

Most companies secure financing through loans from banks that often extend credit accounts. Established companies usually have sizeable credit lines that they can use to draw funds if they need to meet their cash requirements for their operations.

The debt that companies take from banks can be used for purchasing new equipment, stocking more inventory or pay employee wages. Most loans require repayment in a shorter period as opposed to fixed-income securities.

Meanwhile, fixed-income instruments refer to those that are issued by the company and acquired by stock investors. If you buy any form of fixed-income securities, you are fundamentally lending money to the company.

Companies that issue fixed-income instruments are obliged to pay underwriting fees. However, loan securities allow the company to raise money and retain the money for a longer duration as opposed to usual terms.

There will be instances that you will encounter companies who are about to go into debt. This doesn't necessarily mean that you should stay away from these company stocks. In fact, you should take a closer look instead to understand why the company has to take loans. Probably, the company has an important project on the pipeline that if you buy their stocks during pre-launch, you might be in for a treat.

But before you buy the stocks of these companies, there are important considerations that you should take note of.

Company's Current Debt Volume

If the company has minimal debt volume, then taking on some loans may actually be advantageous as it can provide more flexibility for reinvesting its funds into operation or expansion.

But if you have discovered that the company already has a high debt volume, then you need to perform more intensive due diligence. Basically, high debt is not a good indicator because it may affect the ability of the company to create a cash surplus.

The Type of Debt

Fixed-income securities issued by the company and fund influx from external sources have different maturity dates. Some types of debt are short-term (they should be paid no longer than 12 months), while others are long-term (the repayment exceeds 12 months).

Debt securities that the general public can buy commonly have longer repayment periods as opposed to the loans offered by credit organizations such as large banks.

Moreover, long-term debt securities typically have higher interest rates and so you need to assess if the company has the capacity to settle the loan on time. For short-term loans, you need to figure out if the company has the immediate cash to settle the loan.

As a stock dividend investor, you have to assess if the interest rate and the repayment period are suitable for the project or expansion that the company is interested to execute.

Debt Purpose

Why is the company applying for a loan in the first place? Would the company use the fund for a new project with high potential for income generation? Is the company in a bad financial situation that it has to take loans to pay its staff wages or consolidate debts?

You must be cautious in assessing this area before you purchase stocks from companies with a bad record of debt management. This indicates that the company is not capable of meeting its financial dues.

Companies that are regularly refinancing debt may eventually shut down because its expenses might be higher compared to their income. This is a bad indicator if you are looking for dividend revenue.

But in reversal, some companies may not have any other option but to refinance their debt to effectively lower their interest rates. Financial managers often recommend this to decrease debt volume.

Capacity to Pay

Established companies commonly conduct feasibility studies and business plans before they decide to pursue a project. But not all ventures are guaranteed with success.

What if a project fails to achieve its projected income? Even successful companies such as Microsoft and Apple have their share of flopped products.

Part of the due diligence before you invest in stock dividends is to determine if the company is still capable of paying its loans if the project fails. You should take a look at the balance sheet of the company and be sure that it has enough cash flow to meet its financial obligations. It is ideal to choose companies that have diversified revenue streams.

Loan Agreement

In evaluating the company's debt volume, you have to check the fine print to see if there are provisions that could be damaging to your interest as an investor.

For example, some banks implement threshold ratio levels. If any of the ratios fall down this threshold, the bank has the right to compel the company to repay the loan immediately.

The sudden demand can amplify any problem inside the company, which in some instances may lead to the liquidation of assets.

In assessing the debt volume of a company, it is ideal to use financial ratios to compare it to the industry debt volume.

Current Ratio

This ratio will allow you to compare short-term assets and short-term liabilities. The higher the short-term assets compared to liabilities, the better it's capacity to pay off its short-term debt.

Debt Equity Ratio

This will allow you to measure the financial leverage of the company you are evaluating for possible investment.

To determine this ratio, you have to get the quotient of the long-term debt and stockholders equity. This will allow you to take a look at the equity proportions and debt that the company will use to finance its assets.

Quick Ratio

This ratio will allow you to assess the company's ability to pay off its short-term loans without selling any inventory.

Choose companies who have backup plans to manage their increasing debt volume. What is the management's plan for repayment? If you need to evaluate the debt volume of a company, you should ensure that the company is well aware of how the debt could affect its investors, how the debt will be paid, and how long it may take to repay the debt.

Sales Performance

In any business, it all comes down to the company's performance in selling its products or services. Numbers don't lie, and as an investor, you can always rely on the sales number to assess the performance of a company that you are interested to invest in.

To assess the sales performance of a company, you have to look into the Price-Sales Ratio that will allow you to evaluate how the company is using its capital and revenue.

To obtain the Price-Sales Ratio, you have to find the market capitalization of the company and divide it by the gross revenue of the company over the past year. Usually, low Price-Sales Ratio indicates a potential investment.

This number can help you to determine the stock value because this will allow you to see how much the market is valuing each dollar of sales. This ratio can be used to figure out the value of growth stocks that can be converted into revenue.

For example, if you are looking into a company that has low profits, you can easily look for the Price-Sales Ratio to determine if the stock is undervalued or overvalued.

If the Price-Sales Ratio is lower as opposed to other companies in the same industry, buying the stocks is viable because these stocks are more likely undervalued. However, be sure also to check other financial metrics and ratios to validate the proper valuation of the stocks.

With highly cyclical industries such as airlines, there are only specific years that they are producing profits. But this doesn't mean that the airline industry is not a valuable industry to invest with. In this case, you can use the Price-Sales Ratio instead of the Price-Earnings Ratio to figure out how much the company is paying for every dollar of their sales rather than their earnings.

If the company has negative earnings, the ratio can be considered as not an ideal metric to use because the capacity will be restricted to the stock value as the denominator is virtually lower than zero.

The Price-Sales Ratio can be used to confirm that the company's growth has not become overvalued. This can help you in evaluating companies that have minimal earnings. Unless the company is shutting down, the Price-Sales Ratio can be used to figure out if the company stocks are valued lower against other companies in the same industry.

For example, let's say that the company you are looking into has a Price-Sales Ratio of 0.7 while other companies in the same industry have an average of Price-Sales Ratio of 2.0.

If this company succeeds in reviving its cash flow, the shares may experience a significant increase as the ratio will become closely matched with other businesses in the same sector.

Meanwhile, the dividend yield could be affected if a company is suffering a loss. In this case, the Price-Sales Ratio can be used as one remaining metric to value the business. Take note that a low Price-Sales ratio is usually a good sign, while a high Price-Sales Ratio is an indicator that you have to dig deeper.

Company turnover is only considered valuable if it can be converted into earnings. For instance, property development companies have high sales turnover but often retain average profits.

On one hand, a company in the tech industry can easily produce $10 in net profit for every $22 in sales. This margin shows that sales dollars are not an absolute metric for every company.

There are some dividend stock investors who look at sales performance as a more reliable indicator of the growth of the company. Although profits are not always a good signal for financial wealth, sales performance is not always reliable.

Looking into the sales performance of a company must be done with a cautious assessment of the profit margins and always be sure to compare the findings with other companies in the same industry.

Why Look into Company Debt in Assessing Price-Sales Ratio?

The Price-Sales Ratio doesn't usually take into account the debt that is recorded in the company's balance sheet. Companies with zero debt and low Price-Sales Ratio is a good dividend investment as opposed to companies with high debt and the same level of Price-Sales Ratio. The former can easily pay its debt.

As a method for business valuation, the Price-Sales Ratio doesn't consider the fact that companies with high debt will require higher sales to service the debt. But companies that are in danger of liquidation and have high debt volume can still be revived with low Price-Sales Ratio. This usually happens if the company sales have not experienced a decline, while the share price and capitalization are starting to break down.

Some stock dividend investors use this approach to determine the difference between high-debt companies and startup companies. You can also use the enterprise overvalue methods instead of the market cap over sales.

This method includes the long-term debt of the company. In including this figure to the market capitalization of the company and deducting the cash on hand, you can easily determine the value of the business. The business value is then considered as the overall cost of acquiring the company, including the leftover cash and outstanding debt.

Similar to all methods of valuation, sales-based metrics are not an end-all-be-all approach for a business assessment. You should consider other metrics to properly determine the value of a company.

Low Price-Sales Ratio may signify unrealized potential in value as long as other metrics are confirmed such as high-profit margins, low debt volume, and high growth prospects. If you only rely on Price-Sales Ratio alone, you cannot say that you properly valued the company you are interested in dividend investing.

Prevailing Tax Laws for Dividend Investments

Based on a report released by the American Shareholders Association, the number of corporations releasing dividend payouts to their shareholders had been declining for almost 25 years.

This trend was dramatically averted thanks to the passage of the Jobs and Growth Tax Relief Reconciliation Act (JGTRRA) that was passed in 2003 by the US Congress.

On top of other important taxation reforms designed to boost the US economy, this crucial legislation reduced the rate of individual income tax on dividends to 15 % and also reduced the rate of individual income tax on long-term capital gains to only 15 %. However, the JGTRRA includes a sunset provision, which expired in 2011.

After the enactment of JGTRRA, hundreds of American companies increased the number of their dividend payouts. This continued to rise in the early 2000s but was affected during the economic recession in 2008.

Part of your responsibility as a stock dividend investor is to review the prevailing taxation on dividend payouts. This will help you assess how much you have to pay so you can receive substantial income from your dividend investments.

The changes in the dividend taxation influenced by this important legislation were applicable for domestic companies and eligible foreign companies that are operating in the US. It also covers companies that were originally incorporated in a country where particular agreements with the US are recognized.

But the reforms in dividend taxation are not applicable to dividend payouts from the following companies or specific circumstances:

- Companies that were granted an exemption for federal income tax payment

- Short-sale investments that require payment in the form of property

- Credit unions, mutual insurance companies, mutual savings banks, farmer's cooperatives, cemeteries, and other companies that are exempted from paying certain taxes

- Securities owned via employee-employer agreements

- Shares owned not less than 60 days during the 120 days prior and after the confirmation of stocks for ex-dividend date

- Real Estate Investment Trusts (REITs)

Short Overview of US Dividend Tax Rates

It is important for you as a stock investor to learn the background of dividend taxation in the US. This will help you better understand the impact of the JGTRRA legislation.

Taxation began with an initial corporate income tax at a fixed rate of 35%, which was levied against the profits of the company. After paying its tax obligations, the company can decide if it will release dividends to its stockholders.

The income received from dividend payouts was considered as personal income, so it will be subject to taxation again. For the highest taxpayer bracket, the income tax used to hit as high as 39 % from dividends.

Many companies in the US have appealed about the issue of double taxation. Take note that the main goal of companies is to increase the value of their stocks. When companies generate profits, they have the option to pay dividends or reinvest their earnings back to the business.

Remember, dividend payouts are perceived as an inefficient use of profits, so companies are more interested to fund activities that will further increase capital gains, in which shareholders are also taxed but at a lower rate of 20%.

This scenario compelled companies to spend their earnings on stock buyback schemes, R&D, new acquisitions, equipment purchasing, and other expenditures that may help the business further its operations. These activities can boost the company's share price and ultimately can result in bigger gains for investors when they sell their stocks.

But after the enactment of JGTRRA, that situation changed dramatically. The legislation served as the equalizer between various forms of revenue distribution available for publicly traded companies.

Corporate Benefits of JGTRRA

From the company standpoint, dividends are considered as part of the cost of capital. Reducing the dividend tax rates make it a lot cheaper for companies to do business by making it easier for them to pay dividends to their stockholders.

This perspective encouraged companies to invest their revenues on profitable business activities than focusing on opportunities that will allow them to stay away from releasing dividend payouts.

Corporate executives gained huge advantages from the enactment of JGTRRA. Many business leaders received substantial rewards because they are also shareholders of the company, and their shares are substantial and commonly preferred.

Business executives received huge dividend payouts, some of them in millions. And with the JGTRRA, they only had to pay 15 % tax compared to the previous 28%.

Investor Benefits of JGTRRA

Investing in dividend-paying companies like General Electric, Johnson & Johnson, and Coca-Cola has been an effective strategy for stock investors who are looking for regular passive income.

Stock investors consider regular dividend payouts as a strong signal of company performance while abrupt cancellation of dividend payouts is a sign of weakness. So, companies with a consistent record of dividend payouts are more motivated to sustain the payouts.

Stable but slow-growing business organizations are known as widow-orphan stocks because they provide a high-level safety net for investors who are averse to risk.

After the enactment of the JGTRRA, companies that are already paying dividends have become more attractive to investors, particularly for those in the highest tax tiers.

The 15% tax rate on dividend payouts is already a huge help, considering the revenue generated by bonds and other fixed-income instruments are taxed at 28% at most.

Investors in the lower tax tiers also gained a lot of benefits from the reduced tax rates on dividends with the dividend tax rates plummeting to only 5%.

While lower tax rates are direct and immediate, these are not the only benefits for investors. We also need to consider the impact on stock prices if a company announces a new dividend payout. With this news, the stock price of a company will become more attractive to investors, and so the share prices could increase. This trend usually results in larger capital gains for stock dividend investors on top of their dividend payouts.

Apart from monetary benefits, dividend payouts also have benefits in market behavior. Although there is no way to measure this from a financial perspective, the increasing number of companies that are releasing dividend payouts can positively affect the sentiment in the stock market.

While JGTRRA expired in 2010, the US Congress approved the extension of specific provisions. As an investor, you must be careful in placing your investments in a position where you are only expecting an income stream that might be substantially affected because of certain legislations.

Chapter Takeaways

In this chapter, we discussed the six important factors that you should look into before you buy stocks from companies that are paying dividends:

- Dividend Yield

- Profit Growth Rate

- Balance Sheet

- Debt Volume

- Sales Performance

- Prevailing Tax Laws for Dividend Investments

It is not enough to choose stocks of companies because they have a record of paying dividends to their shareholders.

You also need to take a closer look at other metrics such as profit growth rate, balance sheet status, debt volume, sales performance, and prevailing tax laws that could affect your capital gains and dividend payouts.

Assessing certain dividend stocks against these metrics will ensure that you are investing in high-potential instruments.

Aside from these metrics, you also need to follow proven strategies in choosing stocks for your dividend investments.

In this book, we will look at two proven strategies - high dividend growth rate strategy and high dividend yield strategy.

In the next chapter, we will first explore the high dividend growth rate strategy.

Chapter 4 - Stock Dividend Strategy: High Dividend Growth Rate

"Earning money is not a sin, and the bottom line is growth."

- Rohit Shetty

In order to win in dividend investing, you must follow a game plan that will guide you which stocks to buy and when it is time to sell.

One common strategy used by successful stock dividend investors is called the High Dividend Growth Rate Strategy (HGDRS).

The basic premise of HGDRS is acquiring stocks of companies that are currently paying lower dividend payouts but are growing at a rapid rate that within the immediate future (five to 10 years), the capital gains will be immense.

While companies that are paying high dividend payouts have performed quite well in the market, many of them are now expensive to acquire if you assess it using common valuation metrics.

Although these companies might still be capable of paying high dividends, the low-interest rate in recent years pushed many of them to go into debt to finance their expansion projects. When the interest rates increased, most of these companies are struggling to service the debt.

Meanwhile, companies with consistent records of growing their dividends may present attractive investment opportunities despite the potential volatility in the prices and rising interest rates.

Choosing companies that are growing their dividends will provide you the opportunity to own high-quality shares that you can convert into cash in the immediate future. This will let you set buffer against the volatility in the market and mitigate the risk for rate increases.

This investment strategy goes beyond the common game plan for choosing domestic large-capital stocks. But this is proven effective for choosing small to medium capital stocks that can be used for global stock portfolios.

Why Choose Companies with High Dividend Growth Rate?

When it comes to earnings and leverage, growth-oriented stocks have a tendency to be of better quality as opposed to the stocks in the wider market. In general, if a company has the capacity to boost its dividend payouts for years, it is a strong signal that it has financial strength and discipline.

On the other hand, a high dividend payout is not always a reliable indicator that the company has financial discipline and strength. There are cases when new companies tried to attract investors by taking debt just to increase their payouts.

High-dividend payers with better financial leverage, but lower profitability and earnings growth have the tendency to decrease or cancel their dividends during intense volatility in the market.

Growth focused dividend stocks are ideal for investors who are looking for stable companies that can withstand any market conditions, specifically during bear markets.

Due to its focus on increasing the dividend rate instead of yield, the performance of dividend growers is less affected by the value factor as opposed to high dividend payers. If the stock market follows a growth trend, the performance of growth-focused stocks will not be significantly affected.

Unlike most yield-focused stocks that tend to focus on sectors like utilities, staples, and finance, growth stocks are composed of diversified industries. So the sector composition of a growth-focused dividend portfolio is more stable in the long-term. Diversification is a good practice in most stock investments.

Because of the focus on healthy balance sheets, growth-oriented stocks are recommended to investors who are averse to volatility and increasing interest rates but are still looking to hold shares that will provide them passive income. If you like this arrangement, HGDRS seems a good fit for you.

Based on hypothetical stocks analysis, growth-focused stocks may easily generate more income over time as opposed to stocks with higher yield but average or even slower dividend growth.

While the yield on growth-focused stocks is lower compared to yield-focused stocks, an increasing dividend and rising share price may lead to more stable returns in the long run.

For example, let's say that you are choosing stocks of two companies that you want to include in your dividend portfolio.

- Company P has a dividend yield of 3.7% and has a track record of increasing the dividend by at least 4% annually and the present dividend payout ratio is at 58%.

- Company Q has a dividend yield of 0.90% but its growth rate is at 19%. The present dividend payout ratio is 11%.

Considering other metrics are normal, most investors would choose Company Q if they are looking for a high dividend growth rate. Company P appears to be a better option, but if you choose Company Q, you may end up cashing in compounded dividend revenues when you hold Company Q stocks because the growth can be sustained in the next five to 10 years.

As dividends increase alongside profits, the yield-on-cost starts to overtake the company with minimal growth.

Gradually, the core business may reach its ultimate potential and most of the surplus generated annually may be enough for reinvestment on top of dividend payout. If you achieve this milestone, shareholder-friendly business management will release the extra profits to the owners either through dividend payouts or share buyback scheme.

One example is McDonald's Corporation who conquered each state in the US through franchising during its early years of doing business. During that time, the dividends were minimal. However, investors who had purchased their shares during that time were able to cash in huge dividend payouts when the business expanded.

Stock investors 30 to 40 years ago who followed the HGDRS would find it difficult to let go of their blue-chip holdings today.

Why Dividend Growth Is an Important Metric?

Which of the two business scenarios will provide you peace of mind?

- Holding stocks of a company that is paying you large dividend today and is experiencing a gradual decline in its core business

- Holding stocks of a company that is paying a small dividend today but enjoys higher revenue year after year

If you think there's a level of safety net in a company, you may want to consider HDGRS, because this is a wiser game plan.

Companies are not motivated to increase their dividend payouts if they cannot sustain it for the next decade.

Therefore, an increasing dividend rate on a per-share basis is a common indicator of a vote of confidence from the people who have seen and evaluated the balance sheet and income statement of the company.

Dividend Growth Investing

Like any investment strategy, HGDRS is not a failproof game plan mainly because of the inherent risks that are present in the stock market. For example, the biggest risk in this strategy is a macro movement that is way beyond your control. This pertains to the interest rate in the market.

Warren Buffet refers to the interest rate as financial gravity because it appears to be the universal force in the financial world. The interest rates determined by the government can influence all financial assets that individuals and companies can pay before securing income streams like earnings, dividends, and interest income.

If you analyze the historical insights, the P/E stocks today are in wild levels as opposed to the dividend rates that are still considered minimal. This is mainly because of the current policy of the US Federal Reserve that pushes down the yield on all government bonds to minimal rates.

Essentially, the short-term government bonds are regarded as a representation of the risk-free interest rate that you can earn your income. So, all other assets are relatively priced to these federal bonds. If the interest rates of the bonds are quite low, the majority of investors will turn to financial instruments that can provide better yields like stocks.

The minimal interest rate on government bonds has been prevailing for at least two decades now, which has been beneficial for investors. As the interest rates fall, the share price and bonds have increased, which caused the progress in the stock and market bond.

But eventually, interest rates will increase and becomes problematic. If the long-term trend leans toward lower dividend yield, then the interest rate will still follow a cycle of rising and falling to balance the inflation. This is important for the national economy and way beyond your control. All you can do is to be on alert as with interest rates at an all-time low, the only path it could follow is upwards.

For example, let's say you need to analyze a federal 20-year bond that yields 2% yearly and stock from Company R that has a share price of $98. You have discovered that similar to the federal bonds, the Company R profits have been stagnant, but its financial position is quite strong, so its dividend yield is sustained at 4%.

It is important to tackle this tradeoff if you are making an investment decision. If you are looking for a higher dividend yield, you would certainly go with Company R stocks. However, if you want a steady stream of interest payouts, the federal bonds are a good choice.

But what will happen if the dividend yield of the federal bond increases to 4%? Both the Company R stocks and the federal bonds can yield the same amount. With these options, which would you choose for your portfolio?

Given the same growth rate and the higher risk in Company R's profits, you can go for federal bonds. If you take a closer look, there is no real advantage in choosing Company R stocks, and the risk is actually higher.

If the government decides to increase the rates, most investors will be less interested to pay for non-federal bonds or stocks. Stock prices will eventually plummet to rectify the relative stock valuation. So, the dividend yield of Company R should increase its size by twice the amount to recover the proper valuation as opposed to federal bonds.

There's a chance that the stock price would be reduced by 50%. Investors who purchased Company R stocks would have lost the same points of their investments. And more often than not, the decline will be short-term, and so it may take a long while before they can recover their investment.

As of press time, the federal bond yield is at 2.35% and the dividend growth stocks can't provide higher yields. Investors who have invested in yield-focused stocks may lose a lot of money if the government decides to increase the rates.

Risks in Using HGDRS as Investment Strategy

Most growth-oriented stocks have increased their share prices as investors are expecting a steady stream of increasing dividend payouts. However, there's still an inherent risk when the company fails to succeed in increasing the share prices.

Companies, even those that are already stable organizations, are managed by executives who are still susceptible to committing errors in judgment.

For instance, Best Buy was among the most high-potential growth-focused companies in the last decade. If you take a look at its track record, you can see that it has remarkable profit and growth. The company's balance sheet was outstanding and was even implementing a buyback program.

But in 2006, the company's growth started to go south, and its performance changed into losses. The stock price significantly declines from $60 to just $12 in 2012. Stockholders lost about 80% of their investment and the company is still struggling to recover its loss as of press time.

Sadly, Best Buy is not the only company to have gone through such an ordeal. There are many more companies who have experienced significant declines in performance. Based on a study conducted by financial analysts from Yale University, the average lifespan of a company listed in the S&P 500 declines from 67 years in the 1920s to just 15 years in 2016.

Among the main reasons why companies are delisted in the S&P 500 is due to financial constraints. In 2016, around 44 companies in the index settled more than 100% of their Earnings Per Share that was a record high in more than a decade.

Financial analysts today believe that the growth of dividends over the years will slow down by 45%, which is an early signal of financial distress.

Furthermore, there are more companies today that are no longer capable of investing in assets that are profit-generating. The typical approach today is to use the cash flow to reduce shareholder equity. This can easily boost the profits on paper, but this has certain limits. The stock price performance that is reducing dividends is often not good.

Investing in growth-oriented stocks precludes high margins of safety that could be helpful in protecting against a decline in performance. Remember, the core of this strategy is on growth and not so much on security that requires a strong safety net.

There's a limit on growth-oriented stocks, and by focusing on expected growth, you might be placing your investment at a huge risk.

Choose Companies with Strong Competitive Advantages

If your eye is fixated on holding a regular stream of increasing dividends, then at least choose companies who have solid competitive advantages.

Companies who don't have a strong competitive advantage have the tendency to revert to a regular range of growth and revenue, and the value of the stock may be affected.

This phenomenon is quite common in the stock market and this is called by Warren Buffer as the reversion to the mean.

Competitive advantages will eventually fade over time. Buffett calls these as moats that are not absolute protection for a castle. New technologies, business processes, or products will be developed that could disrupt your core business.

Companies like Coca Cola, Harley Davidson, and Google have strong moats. But the stocks of these companies are really high today.

Chapter Takeaways

In this chapter, we have learned the following takeaways:

- HGDRS is one approach that you can use so you can narrow down your investment and focus only on companies that are growth-oriented.

- The stocks of growth-focused companies that are still performing today are known as the survivors. These organizations stood the test of time and had been paying dividends to their shareholders.

- The survival of a growth-focused company over several years is mostly driven by moats. The previous performance of the company has minimal effect on its present business.

Some dividend investors are more interested in higher payouts instead of growth. We'll explore this game plan in the next chapter.

Chapter 5 - Stock Dividend Strategy: High Dividend Yield

"Buy into good, well-researched companies and then wait. Let's call it a sit-on-your-hands investment strategy." - Kenneth Fisher

High Dividend Yield Strategy (HDYS) is another major approach used by stock dividend investors. This game plan typically leads to substantial cash income from slow-growth companies but are releasing high dividend payouts.

But too much focus on payout alone may obscure the actual essence of long-term stock investing that includes income and capital growth.

Remember, HDYS is a strategic approach in trading stocks in which the investors are mainly concerned about the dividend payouts. This approach also prefers stock valuation because this is really the low price of the stock relevant to the dividend that primarily causes the high yield.

HDYS is just one strategy you can follow in stock dividend investing that can help you in choosing stocks. There are also theories and strategies that point out to the probability that the capital gain can outperform growth in long-term investment. As such, the dividend yield in HDYS really points out to the value premium.

Other investment strategies concentrate on stocks based on high cash flow or high earnings relevant to the stock price and the equity's high book value. Basically, HDYS only produces minimal yield because the stocks are chosen from a pool composed of established companies.

Investors who are following the HDYS do not invest in companies that are not issuing dividends. They are willing to forego the possible increase in the share price and would instead prefer to receive regular payouts. Furthermore, company stocks that are selected based on their high dividend yield usually show strong performance in the stock market, which affects the share price of the company that is crucial for capital gains.

However, there are also stock investors who choose stocks from companies that are generating enough profits but have significantly decreased their dividend payouts or have temporarily suspended the dividend release.

Bear in mind that there is no single dividend investing strategy that can outperform consistently over shorter time periods. Hence, diversifying your investments can be beneficial at this point, particularly for individuals who are actually traders and not investors.

One primary benefit of selecting high-dividend stocks is that they are not highly volatile. However, company stocks based on earnings or cash flow have a moderately higher risk. HDYS may lead to less stock turnover as opposed to a game plan that is based on cash flow or profits, and in this case, it can dramatically reduce capital gains tax.

However, an investing strategy that adheres to high book-to-market may also reduce turnover and capital gains tax. If you focus on consistent income generation, HDYS is not considered tax-efficient, especially if you are trading in a country with higher dividend tax rates than the US.

HDYS is normally attractive to the natural desires of dividend investors to hold on to their equities. Company stocks chosen through this strategy are usually stable and strong enough to outperform the stock market even during volatile markets.

But HDYS may not be applicable to wealthy investors or high-income earnings because this strategy may just lead to unnecessary income that will only create tax drag on wealth accumulation.

You might be better off building a revenue stream using a systematic withdrawal scheme from a stock portfolio that attracts better returns from other investment strategies instead of relying solely on HDYS.

The Pros of Following HDYS as an Investment Strategy

Most companies that are paying dividend payouts are in the defensive sectors that are naturally capable of sustaining economic turmoil. These companies usually have considerable cash reserves, so they can easily sustain the dividend payouts even if their profits are affected by negative economic activities.

The dividend yield is a metric that you can use to help you determine how much per share a company is currently paying its shareholders per year in the form of the dividend. This is written as a percentage.

Remember, you can determine the dividend yield by getting the quotient of the annual dividend per share and the price for each share.

Stock investors can mainly benefit from dividends as a source of regular passive income, which they can further use to reinvest back in the company. This is a common practice in stock investing.

Some investors often choose dividend stocks so they have another source of passive income that they can use during retirement. Aside from the dividend payout, investors can also make money through the appreciation of the share price.

Many of the companies that are paying dividends have existing dividend reinvestment plans that will allow you to use your dividends in buying more stocks from the company. This will let you gradually build your investment portfolio that can have substantial value in the long run.

In chapter 9, we will explore reinvestment plans in detail. But for now, you should know that many companies are now offering reinvestment plans because they want to leverage the existing pool of long-term investors who believe in the future of the company.

As mentioned earlier, most companies that are issuing dividend payouts are in defensive sectors. These companies are often non-cyclical organizations and they do not depend on the conventional economic cycles.

Defensive companies are strong enough to withstand negative economic trends and their stocks are less volatile as opposed to other stocks on the market. This is ideal for investors who want to stay away from too much risk. These stocks can pay higher than the amount that the investors usually receive from conservative instruments like federal bonds.

Companies in the defensive sectors include food, housing, utility, pharmaceuticals, and healthcare. Even during economic recessions, people still need to buy food, keep the lights on, and buy medicine when they are sick.

Most companies that are issuing dividend payouts are stable companies with a proven track record in the stock market. They have the financial capacity to issue dividends to investors because they usually have enough cash reserves. Examples of these companies are Procter & Gamble and Coca Cola who pay in the range between 3% to 4% dividends per annum.

Eventually, stable companies perform better. According to a study published by Forbes Magazine in 2015, companies that are paying dividends have performed well since the 1920s. The average yearly growth of non-dividend stocks is 8.5% while the average yearly growth of dividend stocks is 10.4%.

Dividend stocks are also significantly less volatile with an average deviation at 18% as opposed to the 30% deviation recorded for non-dividend stocks.

The Cons of Following HDYS as an Investment Strategy

There are two major risks in following HDYS as an investment strategy:

1. Variable interest rate

2. Unguaranteed dividend payouts

Investing in high dividend stocks can be an amazing opportunity for stock market investors who are looking to earn significant dividend payouts while enjoying the possible appreciation of their holdings.

However, it requires proper and comprehensive due diligence to ensure that the stocks will yield substantial payouts.

Remember, HDYS works by selecting stocks that are managed by highly-qualified business executives on top of healthy balance sheets. There are cases of companies that have an outstanding record of paying dividends but were heavily affected by poor market conditions or short-term problems in the company. These activities usually affect the release of dividend payouts, which can derail the overall objective of HDYS.

Take note that dividend stocks may be affected by the performance of the business as well as the prevailing interest rates. For example, if interest rates increase, dividend payouts may not be that enticing to investors. This may lead to the selling of stocks or equity outflows.

The majority of high dividend stocks are in consumer staples, REITs, utilities, and limited partnerships. Large-cap indexes such as Dow Jones and S&P 100 are also composed of high dividend yield stocks.

High Dividend as a Possible Signal for Underlying Business Problems

While stocks with high dividend payouts are usually enticing for investors, not all are worthy of investments. In some cases, a high dividend payout could be an indicator that a company is struggling.

If you only choose stocks solely on the basis of dividend payouts, you might be at risk of losing your investment when the stock price plummets or if dividend payouts are significantly reduced.

Remember, the stock market is considered a forward-looking market and normally doesn't consider the internal struggles of a company. As a dividend investor, it becomes your responsibility to know more about the business organization that you are eyeing for possible investment.

Let's say that Company S is trading at $100 and releases $5 per share as an annual dividend payout. Therefore, its dividend yield is at 5%. But some market movement resulted in a loss of the company's earnings capacity. The share price of the company goes south until it hits $50 within a week, which is a staggering 50% loss. Because the dividend payout is released annually, the figures of Company S will show that its dividend yield is still $5 per share, which is now at 10%.

However, this high dividend yield is considered temporary as the typical factors that cause the decline of share prices may also lead to a reduction in dividend payout. Company S may even decide to sustain the dividend as a reward for its shareholders for not selling their stocks.

But you should not forget to look into the operations as well as the financials of the company before you purchase its stocks. This will definitely help you figure out if the dividend payouts are sustainable.

Aside from operations and financials, you should specifically look into the company's free cash flow, a record of payout ratio, a record of dividend payout schedules, and the strategic plan.

The majority of high dividend companies are considered "Blue Chip Companies" who are known to withstand economic downturns and can even record positive profits and growth amidst economic turmoil.

The Role of Interest Rate in HDYS

Dividend Yield is still susceptible to the decision of the government to implement stricter financial control.

And so, many stock dividend investors evaluate their potential investment in a company relative to the prevailing interest rate.

If the interest rates increase, it may result in outflows in dividend payouts but may cause share prices to plummet.

Significant changes in the prevailing interest rates may trigger some movements in the market and may cause the market to become bearish.

Therefore, it is crucial to always check the current interest rates and read the latest financial news to figure out if there are possible changes looming ahead.

To provide you a perspective, the US government has been continuously increasing the interest rates since 2015. This trend is currently affecting the decades of bullish returns in the stock market.

On top of the increasing interest rates, the inflation rate has been rising. But despite these financial movements, the US stock market is still a lucrative market, thanks to the improving economy (better than 2008) and the gradual recovery of the labor market.

Chapter Takeaways

In this chapter, we have learned the following:

- Now might be a good time to check the current roster of companies that are paying high dividends.

- HDYS may provide you to gain leverage of the higher risk-free rate in liquid cash savings. But you may choose to balance out your dividend stocks with short-term fixed bonds.

- HGDRS and HDYS will serve as your game plan in choosing the dividend stocks for your investment portfolio.

If you think you are now ready to take your pick, then let's explore that in the next chapter.

Chapter 6 - Choosing Dividend Stocks for Your Investment Portfolio

"The reality is that business and investment spending are the true leading indicators of the economy and the stock market. If you want to know where the stock market is headed, forget about consumer spending and retail sales figures. Look to business spending, price inflation, interest rates, and productivity gains." - Mark Skousen

By now, you must understand that investing in stock dividends is a slow but sure approach towards generating passive income and accumulating wealth.

When you invest in dividend stocks, you can expect regular dividends in the form of cash or additional stocks. And as long as you hold on to your equity, you can benefit from a potential appreciation of stocks as the company performs well in the stock market.

Warren Buffet is probably one of the most popular stock market investors today. He is the CEO of Berkshire Hathaway and earned the nickname the Oracle of Omaha because of his savvy investing strategies and practices. One of them is investing in Blue Chip company stocks that are paying dividends.

Buffett is also known for his strategy of reinvesting his dividends instead of cashing out the payouts. This strategy is an effective approach in stock market investing as the dividends may provide you a safety net against inflation. This safety net is virtually non-existent if you invest in fixed-rate federal bonds.

Many beginners in stock dividend investing usually have the impression that investing in stock dividends is easy. After all, you just need to narrow down your options to companies that are paying dividends, right? Then instead of cashing out the dividends, you just need to reinvest them into the company so you can continue accumulating your wealth.

However, it is never that easy. You must ensure that you are investing in companies with outstanding traction and are well-positioned to perform well within its industry or sector, and in the stock market in general.

So how can you choose which dividend stocks to buy for your investment portfolio? Here are some pointers to consider.

Consistent Cash Flow

Cash is king! The number one criteria that you should look into whenever you are choosing dividend stocks is the cash flow of the company.

Choose companies that have consistent positive cash flow and set aside those companies with a record of inconsistency.

It can be easy to see healthy dividend returns from companies that can provide you with regular passive income. There are many companies that are growing and are also consistently profitable, so it is best to stick with them.

Be steadfast in this factor and only select profitable companies that also demonstrate growth. The ideal long-term profit growth is between 5% and 15%. It may not be wise to go beyond this range as there are possibilities of disappointments that could affect the share price.

While profitability can drive growth and will always be a crucial indicator of a quality dividend-paying business, you must always remember that dividends can be extracted from the cash flow of the company. As such, you should assess if the company has enough supply of cash.

You must also choose companies that have increased their dividend payouts within the last five years. This can dramatically increase the odds of consistent dividend increase that is, of course, a huge benefit for you as an investor.

Stay Away from Companies with Too Much Debt

As much as possible, avoid choosing companies with too much debt. How can you verify this criterion? You can do so by looking at the Debt-Equity Ratio of the company. The ideal ratio is 1.00, and if the ratio hits 2.0, just look elsewhere.

This is actually a no-brainer in stock trading. If the company has too much debt, then it will be compelled to settle its dues first before paying dividends. When the debt becomes due, the company has to raise the funds to service the debt. This can easily affect the volume and frequency of dividend payouts.

Aside from the Debt-Equity Ratio, you should also check the Debt-Capital ratio of the company. Taking on loans is often inevitable in business. The company may need an additional cash influx to fund expansion or acquisition.

If you have struggled with student loans or high mortgage, you will certainly understand that loans can put a lot of strain on the family budget. If you have kids and they are asking for an extra allowance, would you be able to grant that, considering you have loans to pay?

The same is true for businesses regardless of the industry or size. If a business has loans to pay, it will struggle to sustain its dividend payouts. This is the main reason why you must take a closer look at the Net Debt-Capital Ratio of the company. This will help you determine how much debt the business is using to fund its operations.

Let's say that Company T has recently acquired an important piece of equipment to upgrade its manufacturing process. The equipment is worth $50 Million, and you want to know if the business has paid the equipment in cash or through financing.

You can determine the percentage of the company's financing by looking at the Debt-Capital Ratio. You later found out that the equipment was purchased by 60% cash from the company and 40% financing.

It is best to choose stocks from a company with Debt-Capital Ratio that is not higher than 50%. But remember that some sectors such as utilities are typically into high debt levels because of the stability of their profits.

If a business suddenly declines due to market movements and has high debt volume, the share price can be significantly affected, and the dividend payout will be at risk.

Check Industry or Sector Health

Some stock dividend investors usually ignore the importance of checking the health of the industry or sector before buying stocks.

At present, the banking industry in the US is in a bit of a struggle due to the extra regulation, as well as emerging disruptive technology such as digital banking, mobile payments, and even cryptocurrencies.

Share prices of some financial companies are on a trade-off, and because of the fading demand in this sector, a substantial increase in dividend payouts, as well as stock price appreciation, may not happen in the immediate future.

On the other hand, the demand for aged care services will continue to increase in the next 20 to 30 years due to the aging population in the US.

While this doesn't completely guarantee that the stocks in the healthcare sector will not be susceptible to market movements, it increases the odds for these companies to be stronger as opposed to other sectors. As long as the industry or sector is booming, there is always a chance for the dividend stocks to appreciate.

Some investment advisors would tell you to check on the history of the stocks so you can assess its potential for growth. While it is somehow important, relying completely on the historical record of a particular stock will be half-baked assessment.

Consider the case of companies like Coca Cola and Pepsi who have enjoyed significant revenue and growth in the last century by selling sugared water. But with the rise of health consciousness among consumers, investing in these companies may not guarantee the same success in the future.

The major players in the soda industry are now gradually shifting into alternative drinks, but it may take some time before they catch up with the demand. Instead of relying on this factor that is way beyond your control, choose stocks of companies that are highly predicted to boom in the near future.

Select Companies with Highly Qualified Business Executives

You must choose companies that are being driven by business executives who have outstanding performance, unwavering discipline, and commitment to excellence. Business leaders largely play an important role in the creation of wealth for shareholders.

It might overwhelm you to really get to know if a company has the best team. But it is really important to put your investment to people who can really execute and drive the company to success.

In order to do this, you must compare the performance of the company as opposed to other companies in the same industry in a period of at least five years. Moreover, you must also see how the company has performed in leading market indexes.

More often than not, the stock price will manifest if the company has been doing well under its present executive team.

It will also help a lot if you can pinpoint companies who have decided to implement buyback programs when their shares were trading below the average value. This practice usually helps in increasing shareholder value when the share prices start to increase again as this may decrease the number of shares in the market. This is often a strong signal that the people behind the company are loyal to the core of their organization.

On the other hand, you must be cautious about companies that are acquiring companies that are not within their area of expertise. This might be an indicator that the management is overreaching to expand the business.

Choose Companies with Strong Value Proposition

It is common for young investors to be attracted by dividend stocks that are "booming" based on its market price. But experienced investors are usually cautious about this because it would appear that you are chasing the market and not the company.

In fact, there are savvy investors that invest in dividend-paying companies whose stocks are trading below their average value. And many of these investors are looking for companies who have a strong value proposition.

Businesses who are really delivering valuable products and services to their customers have a tendency to be more consistent over time. You must evaluate each business according to its merits. Aside from the payout, a lower share price can provide you with the opportunity to take advantage of possible capital appreciation in the future.

At first, it seems a bad decision to invest in a company whose share price declines during unpredictable movements in the stock market. But if you can really see that the value proposition of the company will continue to be relevant in the next 20 to 30 years, you may ignore the present market condition.

In fact, the ideal time to purchase company stocks is when their share price is reduced. As a dividend investor, you must know how to study the market activities that could have negative effects on the company or its industry.

You should assess if depreciating the share price could reflect the entire value of the company. It might be a great time to buy these stocks while they are still trading below their actual value.

Avoid Companies with High Dividend Yields

It is best to stay away from companies that are offering more than 10% dividend yields if the market average is around 4.5%. This is a strong signal that the market has a general perception that the company's present payout ratio and its dividends are not sustainable.

Bear in mind that the yield is sourced out from the record of dividend payouts over the full financial year as a percentage of the current stocks. It doesn't mean that a company is capable of sustaining its dividend payouts just because it has a history of paying dividend levels in the past. A falling share price might be a reflection of the market expectation for lower dividends in the near future.

Declining share prices may also indicate that the business is implementing dividend recapitalization, which refers to accessing debt instruments to fund dividend payouts for shareholders.

Be sure to look at the cash record of the company in the last five years so you can narrow down your list by eliminating companies that have been using debt just to sustain their payouts. With this, you may also determine how much of the dividend is sourced out from the company's own cash reserve.

Choose Well-Established Companies

Basically, dividend-paying companies are considered established business organizations because they typically provide basic necessities such as food, water, gas, housing, and hygiene products. So the common sectors for dividends are as follows:

- Telecommunications

- Energy

- Utilities

- Food

- Clothing

- Toiletries

- Finance

- Real Estate

More often than not, people will still buy these products and avail of these services regardless of the market conditions.

Companies that are less stable are those corporations that provide products or services that are considered not priorities for most people such as computers, cellphones, music, restaurants, and travel.

But this is not always the case. Certainly, many were affected during the market recession of 2008. But the warning indicators were already apparent even prior to the bursting of the bubble. Savvy investors who were knowledgeable of reading those signs bailed out early.

In general, companies that are paying regular dividends are considered more established as opposed to companies that are not paying dividends. In fact, paying dividends is considered as an important factor that helped some companies survive the recession even without government bailout.

It is common among dividend investors to think that more established companies are releasing a big percentage of their profits in the form of dividends because there are limited investment opportunities that can provide decent revenues in their common business areas. But this is not always the case.

For example, General Electric (GE) is one of the most established companies in the world. It has been increasing its dividend payouts and at the same time has been investing a hefty percentage of its revenues to diversify and expand. It has developed and presently operates several business lines from jet aircraft engines, medical equipment, and home appliances.

Consider Investing in Blue Chip Companies

The Standard & Poor's (S&P) 500 is a great place to hunt for dividend-paying companies. This index is composed of the top 500 companies that are performing well and have been evaluated based on specific criteria.

The S&P committee selects well-established companies that can be considered by investors who are after regular returns with minimal risks.

Currently, the best performing stocks in the index are the following:

- Global Payments (GPN)
- FleetCor Technologies (FLT)
- Dentsply (XRAY)
- AMD (AMD)
- Celgene (CELG)
- Synchrony (SYF)
- MSCI (MSCI)
- Align Technology (ALGN)
- Cadence Design Systems (CDNS)
- Tyson Foods (TSN)
- Xerox (XRX)
- Hess Corporation (HESS)
- Anadarko Petroleum (APC)
- Chipotle Mexican Grill (CMG)
- Coty Inc (COTY)

Be Careful in Choosing Speculative Companies

There are companies that are quite new in the stock market and so they are still not listed in any index. These are known as speculative companies.

Even though there is always the possibility to gain considerable returns, there is also a huge risk that you may lose your investments.

Speculative stocks are best reserved for dividend investors who have been in the market for several years, and for those investors who already have the resources to risk their investments.

Another point to consider is that there are only a handful of speculative companies in the US that are paying dividends.

Invest in Sectors You Really Know

If you are just beginning your journey in dividend investing, it is best to start in a sector that you really understand. If you are familiar with the sector or the industry, you are in a much better position to evaluate the companies in the sector.

Basically, the US economy and the stock market are divided into two major categories:

1. Upper Tier (Sector)

2. Lower Tier (Industry)

The Upper Tier is a broad category of companies that have similar economic attributes. There are 11 primary sectors today that you can use to break down the companies you are evaluating.

The Lower Tier refers to the industries that comprise the sectors. Looking at this tier will allow you to narrow down the groups of companies who are in the same business or are catering to the same types of market.

For example, discount retail store Dollar Tree and luxury jeweler Tiffany & Co. are from the same sector (consumer discretionary) but they are different industries.

Looking at sectors and industries will enable you to easily compare one company as opposed to its competitors. There's no sure way to know if a particular dividend stock company is ideal for investment unless you benchmark it against its competitors.

Evaluating sectors and industries can also help you understand how different companies relate to each other.

For example, if you believe that the energy sector will be in a struggle soon, you might instead focus on transport stocks because gasoline will virtually be among the biggest cost inputs.

The ability to read the dynamics of industries and sectors on top of using the most effective dividend investing strategy can help you build your wealth.

Here are the 11 sectors that you should look into:

Sector	Industries	Remarks
Financials	• Banking • Investment Funds • Insurance • Real Estate	The bulk of the revenue generated by this sector comes from mortgages and loans that gain value through interest rates.
Materials	• Mining • Refinery • Chemicals • Forestry	Most companies in the Materials Sector are positioned at the beginning of the supply chain. Therefore, these are highly sensitive to the changes in the business cycle.

Energy	• Oil • Gas Exploration • Energy Production • Integrated Power • Alternative Energy • Renewable Energy	Energy companies are producing revenue that are dependent on the price of crude oil, natural gas, and other commodities
Utilities	• Water • Gas • Electricity • Integrated Providers	This sector generates regular recurring revenue by charging businesses and residential homes. Companies under the Utilities Sector are usually capable of providing larger dividend payouts as

		opposed to other sectors.
Telecomm unications	<ul><li>Satellite companies</li><li>Internet service providers</li><li>Cable Companies</li><li>Wireless Providers</li></ul>	Telecom companies generate recurring profits from consumers. But some subcategories of this sector and industries are highly vulnerable to rapid changes in communications technology.
Consumer Discretion ary	<ul><li>Consumer Durables</li><li>Apparel</li><li>Consumer Service</li><li>Media</li><li>Retail</li></ul>	Companies under this sector usually take advantage of improving economies specifically when

		purchasing power increases.
Industrial	<ul><li>Manufacturing</li><li>Fabrication</li><li>Construction</li><li>Machinery</li><li>Defense</li><li>Aerospace</li></ul>	The growth in this sector is heavily driven by the demand for construction and manufacturing products like manufacturing equipment and agricultural tools.
Consumer Staples	<ul><li>Food and Beverages</li><li>Non-durable household products</li><li>Personal products</li></ul>	Consumer Staples companies are capable of surviving amidst economic turmoil

Technology	Information Technology Software Development Electronics	Tech companies are driven by the overall status of the economy and upgrade cycles. This sector has experienced significant growth over the years.
Healthcare	Medical Devices Hospital Management Pharmaceuticals Biotechnology	Healthcare companies are both defensive and growth companies as people will always have the need for healthcare products and services.
Real Estate	Retail Property Industrial Property	The main source of revenue of the

	Residential Real Estate	Real Estate Sector comes from capital appreciation, purchases, and rental income. This sector is highly vulnerable to changes in the real estate market and prevailing interest rates.

Making a list of companies that you want to buy stocks from can help you to consider the existing competition and how each company stands to depend on the current scenarios in each sector.

Basically, you have to determine three important things:

1. The company's performance in the market

2. The competitive advantage of the company

3. The growth opportunity of the sector in the next 20 to 30 years

Chapter Summary

In this chapter, we have explored important pointers that can help you narrow down your list of potential company stocks that you can include in your investment portfolio:

- Consistent cash flow

- Debt level

- Sector health

- Business management

- Value proposition

- Dividend yield

- Stable profits

- Blue-chip stocks

- Speculative companies

- Sector familiarity

But before you go around buying stocks and expecting dividend payouts, you should never forego the importance of conducting due diligence.

We'll explore that in the next chapter.

Chapter 7 - The Importance of Due Diligence in Stock Dividend Investing

"I'm a pretty disciplined investor and pretty disciplined buyer. I do my due diligence. I do my homework. I don't waste money." - Bruce Rauner

Choosing stocks to add to your dividend investment portfolio requires a considerable amount of time and effort. A huge part of this is often devoted to research and analysis.

As an individual dividend investor, you are in competition against fund managers and stock market professionals who might have some advantages such as exclusive access to company and market insights.

But if you have the resources and the luxury of time to really make sense of the dividend market and the stock market in general, it will be a lucrative venture. Dividend payouts can provide you with regular passive income, while gradually accumulating your wealth through stock appreciation.

Before we explore the steps on how to conduct company due diligence, let us first discuss the importance of understanding the economic and financial factors surrounding dividend investing.

An Overview of The Current US Economy

It is important for dividend stock investors to make sense of the economy and financial conditions before you fill your investment portfolio with stocks. You need to understand how the movements in the stock market and the overall economy could affect your investments.

To start with, you need access to sources of reliable information. Here are the best places where you can read news and insights about market changes if you are in the US:

The US Federal Reserve Board

This government board regularly publishes the US Financial Stability Report, which can provide you with a summary of the Federal Reserve Board's framework in assessing the status, as well as the resilience of the US financial setting. Aside from this regular report, the board also publishes special economic studies that can help you evaluate specific industries and sectors in the US.

Bank Research Section

Major banks and even stockbrokers in the US usually maintain a research section on their websites. You can read the reports and forecasts posted in these sections so you can better understand the current financial condition in the US.

Business Newspapers / Websites / Magazines

Reading newspapers can provide you with an immediate glimpse of what's happening in the business and financial world. The best business newspapers that you should read regularly are the following:

- Financial Times
- Business Standard
- Investor's Business Daily
- The Wall Street Journal
- The Economic Times
- International Business Times

Aside from business newspapers, you should also check out the business section of reliable newspapers of national and international circulation:

- The New York Times
- The New York Post
- The Washington Post
- Chicago Tribune
- Los Angeles Times
- The Mercury News

You should also read business websites like:

- Forbes
- CNN Money
- Google Finance
- CNBC
- Yahoo Finance

- MSN Money Central

- WSJ

- Bloomberg

Consider subscribing to reputable business magazines such as

- Bloomberg Businessweek

- Entrepreneur

- Inc

- Consumer Reports

- Forbes

- WIRED

- Fortune

- The Economist

Whenever you read the news, try to find updates about the following subjects:

- The US Economy

- Prevailing interest rates

- Stock market sentiment

- Interest rates

- Foreign exchange rates

Company Due Diligence

As a dividend investor, you should remember that the value of your investment will always depend on the health of the companies you have investments with. Therefore, it is important that you perform the necessary due diligence before you start investing in any company.

Due Diligence is the process of investigating a company by verifying all available public information. This involves reviewing all financials aside from other relevant materials that can help you decide if the company is worthy of investment.

In the business world, due diligence is usually performed by companies who are interested to acquire another company. This is usually conducted by equity research analysts, fund managers, investment dealers, or investment analysts.

Dividend investors should also conduct due diligence as an optional pre-investment activity. But investment brokers have the legal obligation to conduct due diligence before they sell dividend stocks. This will safeguard them from being legally liable due to the non-disclosure of material information.

Because of the passage of the Securities Act of 1993, due diligence became a popular business term in the US. Stock market brokers have the duty to totally disclose all information relevant to the stocks that they are offering. Brokers who are found guilty of withholding material information will be held criminally liable.

However, this legal obligation could leave stock market brokers susceptible to unfair prosecution if they fail to conceal materials that they did not even possess at the time of the trade offer.

To avoid such unfair practice, the authors of the Securities Act included a legal remedy that states that as long as the stockbroker conducted due diligence in assessing companies whose stocks they are recommending, and the results have been completely disclosed to investors, they may not be liable for any information not discovered during due diligence.

Step-By-Step Process for Performing Due Diligence

As a private individual investing in stock dividends, you don't have any legal obligation to perform due diligence. But this practice can significantly help you pin down the ideal investments to include in your portfolio.

Apart from dividend stocks, you can also use these steps if you want to conduct due diligence for real estate, debt instruments, franchising opportunities, and other types of investments.

1. Verify Business Capitalization

The first step in conducting due diligence for your possible dividend stock investment is to verify the size of the company based on its capitalization.

In general, the company's market cap will let you evaluate the stock volatility, the potential size of the business, and the equity range of the business.

For example, large-cap companies have a tendency to enjoy from stable profit sources and they usually have diversified investor pool. This stabilizes the volatility in the market.

Meanwhile, small-cap companies may only serve specific market segments and have a tendency to be volatile because of the fluctuations in their earnings and stock price.

The market cap will provide you with interesting insights once you start assessing the revenue of the company.

2. Check Profit Margins

After checking the market cap of the company and verifying that it falls within an acceptable threshold, the next step is to check the profit margins and the general revenue trends.

As a dividend investor, you must understand the ROE, profit margins, and gross revenue of the company. You must also check if the company is expanding or downsizing.

Checking the profit margins will allow you to see if the company's revenue trend is increasing, decreasing, or following an almost stagnant path.

Most dividend investors prefer companies with ROE of 50 or higher. This important detail will be key for the next steps in due diligence.

3. Check the Current Competition

Once you are satisfied with the company's market cap and profit margins, the next step is to check the situation in the industry and the sector and benchmark the company against its competitors.

Take note that every company is partially defined by its competitors so be sure to compare the profit margins of the company against 2 to 3 of its largest competitors.

Looking at the biggest competitor in each line of business may help you in assessing the size of the market for the company's products or services.

<u>Is the company you are eyeing for investment considered as a major player in the industry?</u>

<u>What is the present health of the industry in general?</u>

<u>Is there a possibility that the company's current standing in the industry would significantly change in the next 5 to 10 years?</u>

You can research for answers by reading company profiles. Try visiting each company website and find the page dedicated to potential investors. More often than not, you can easily find the company's financials in the Investor Page.

Before you proceed to the next step, you should fill the unknown details in this step, especially if you are still unsure of the company's business model.

There are cases where further research on the company's competitors will help you to make sense of the company you are considering for investment.

4. Study the Valuation Multiples

After benchmarking the company against its competitors, the next step is to study the following metrics: P/E Ratio, PEGs Ratio, and P/S Ratio.

Make sure to include the numbers not only for your target company but also for its competitors. Highlight any considerable discrepancies that you have discovered between the companies so you can review later.

Many dividend investors discover other possible dividend investments in this step. It is okay to consider other companies, but don't easily let go of the company that you are evaluating because it is still too early.

Studying the P/E ratios can help you form your initial assumptions for the company valuation. While profits could be affected by market volatility, the valuations that are sourced from present estimates or trailing profits could be used as a method to measure the performance of the company's competitors.

You may compare the value stock and the basic growth stock alongside the general market sentiment towards the company.

It is also highly recommended to take a closer look at the net profits of the company within a particular period (typically 5 years).

This is to make certain that you are looking at the recent numbers and the figures you have used to calculate the P/E Ratio are accurate and not affected by temporary market movements.

Remember, the P/E Ratio is not a standalone metric because it should be used alongside P/B Ratio, Enterprise Multiple, and Revenue Ratio. These metrics will help you further evaluate the company aside from taking a quick look at its debt volume, yearly earnings, and balance sheet.

Due to the fact that the range in these numbers usually varies from one industry to another, you should assess the same numbers alongside the company's main competitors.

Finally, assessing the PEG ratio will let you look into the prediction for potential profits in the future and how it compares to the actual profits in the present.

In some market sectors, the PEG ratio might be recorded as lower than 1, while in other sectors, this could be as high as 10 or even more.

Stocks with PEG ratios of 1 or lower are considered fairly valued considering the market condition is normal.

5. Scrutinize Business Management

After confirming the numbers, the next step is to check the people behind the company and how they manage the business.

Are the founders still active in managing the business? Or has the board of directors hired seasoned executives to manage the company?

Remember, the age of the company is an essential factor to consider. More often than not, younger companies are still being managed by founding members.

It is best to read the profiles of the company executives to check their experience and expertise. You can easily find this information on the company website, which is usually located under the About Us section or Meet the Team.

Moreover, you should also check if the founders or company executives are still holding a substantial percentage of stocks. Also, check the volume of floating stocks owned by institutional investors. It is crucial to check because it will show you the level of coverage that the business can leverage on top of other factors that may affect the volumes of the trade market.

Low holdings of business executives could be a warning signal, while high holdings of top business managers are a good indicator.

Shareholders of the company are more confident in the business if the executives also have their own stake in the business.

6. Check the Balance Sheet

Scrutinizing the balance sheet of a company is a complex subject that even merits an entire book. But that level of intensive due diligence is often reserved for mergers and acquisitions.

For stock dividend investments, a mid-level analysis will suffice. Look for the summarized version of the balance sheet and check the assets and liabilities of the company.

Focus on the capacity of the company to part short-term liabilities in cash as well as the volume of long-term debt being held by the company.

High debt volume doesn't mean that the business is not in good shape. This still depends on the company's business model. But don't forget to check the ratings of the company when it comes to short-term bonds.

Also, check if the company has the capacity to generate enough cash to pay its debts and sustain its current dividend payouts. Some sectors are capital intensive while in other sectors, the basic structure is enough to operate at a profit.

Find the D/E ratio of the company to check if the company has positive equity. Then, compare this metric with the competitors of the company so you can better make sense of the business.

Figure out the reason if the numbers in the top line (total assets, total liabilities, and shareholder equity) significantly changed within five years. You can better understand the business situation if you read the footnotes in the financial statements.

The balance sheet may have several red flags at face value, but the situation can be explained further in the footnotes. The company might be funding an important expansion project, preparing a new product line, or just accumulating retained profits.

7. Trace the Stock Price History

One important step in performing company due diligence is looking at both the short-term and long-term price movement of the company stocks.

Trace the pattern of the stock price performance. Has it been choppy, volatile, smooth or steady?

Be sure to also check the stock price in different periods - six months, one year, three years, five years, and 10 years. Is the general trend rising or falling?

This can help you assess what type of revenue experience regular shareholders have seen that can also affect the movement of the stock price in the foreseeable future.

Take note that stocks that are volatile are rarely attractive to long-term investors. If too many shareholders are letting go of the stocks, then it may not be a good investment.

8. Check the Stock Options and the Possibility for Dilution

After tracking back the stock price history, the next step is to check the company's SEC filings and look for the outstanding stock options and the predicted conversion. You should also look into the 10-Q and 100K reports.

The abovementioned resources can help you assess how the stock count may change under different price points. The number may tell you if the company is ready for another round of public offering.

Don't forget to check if the company has been investigated for alleged malpractices such as options backdating.

9. Look for Expert Opinions

Step 9 may require a bit of an extra effort on your side because you have to make sense of the general sentiment of stock market analysts when it comes to the profit growth, revenue, and other projections for at least two years from now.

Try to sniff from online discussions or call your colleagues who have the expertise on market trends that may affect the sector, industry or the company you want to invest with. Be sure to ask for details about the company's new partnerships, joint ventures, intellectual property, or new products or services.

In some cases, news about specific activities of a company attracted you to take a closer look, and in this step, you have to re-assess the possibility of using all the details you have uncovered so far.

10. Study Short-Term and Long-Term Risks

Risk assessment is the final step in performing company due diligence. This is to remind you about the risks that are inherent in investing.

Be sure that you understand all the risks when investing within a specific sector, industry, or company.

Are there current disruptions in the sector that you are considering? For example, the rise of cryptocurrencies is seen to cause some changes in the financial sector.

As a dividend investor, you should think ahead to determine the possible worst-case scenarios that could affect your investment.

Will the company survive if a stronger company introduces a better product?

Always ask questions and try to discuss your concerns with your colleagues before investing in any stock dividend.

Chapter Takeaways

In this chapter, we have learned the following steps in conducting company due diligence:

1. Verify business capitalization
2. Check profit margins
3. Check the current competition
4. Study the valuation multiples
5. Scrutinize business management
6. Check the balance sheet
7. Trace the stock price history
8. Check the stock options and possibility for dilution
9. Look for expert opinions
10. Study short-term and long-term risks

As a private individual dividend investor, you are not legally obliged to perform due diligence before you invest in dividend stocks.

You can ignore it completely, but you might be facing a huge risk.

Even seasoned investors are still conducting their due diligence, especially if they are interested to include dividend stocks from companies within a sector they never invested in before.

Plus, conducting due diligence will help you gain experience, and gradually understand the dynamics of stock dividend investing.

Due diligence is also crucial for another strategy that most successful dividend investors are using. They diversify their investment portfolio. Why? Let's explore that in the next chapter.

Chapter 8 - Why Diversification is Essential in Dividend Investing?

"The future is always coming up with surprises for us, and the best way to insulate yourself from these surprises is to diversify." - Robert J. Shiller

Diversifying your investment is a proven method to manage risk in stock dividend investing.

The fundamental concept behind this investment strategy is the theory that diversifying stocks in a portfolio can reduce the risk and can yield higher profits in the long run.

Diversifying your investment portfolio may mitigate the unsystematic risk events so the stocks that are performing well can counter the bad performance of other stocks.

The advantages of diversification are often realized only if the stocks are not related with each other or are from different sectors.

Residual Risk

Also known as unsystematic risk, residual risk is a type of risk that is inherent in an industry or business. This includes the possibility of competitors introducing new products or services that could eat up the market share of companies you have investments with.

While you can predict the sources of the residual risk, there's no way to know the effects of the risk to your investment.

For example, if you buy stocks of companies dealing with the needs of retirees, you are probably aware that significant reforms in the retirement policy in the US could affect your investments. But there's no sure way to know in advance the specifics of the new policies and how the aged care industry and the market will respond.

Stock market studies have shown that diversifying your investment portfolio to at least 25 stocks can significantly reduce the risk. Including securities in your investment could further diversify your portfolio, but the returns might be smaller than usual.

Some dividend investors also diversify their portfolio by including foreign stocks as they will not be affected by the movements in the domestic economy.

For example, a financial recession in the US, may not significantly affect the economy of Japan. Therefore, including Japanese stocks in your portfolio can provide you with an extra layer of protection against the possible losses caused by any adverse movements in the American economy.

Many beginners in stock dividend investing have limited capital. This is a major obstacle in building a diversified and well-balanced portfolio.

An alternative is through mutual funds, in which stockbrokers can offer you diversified stocks based on your investment preferences and risk tolerance.

The Importance of Diversifying Your Portfolio

If you pour all your investment capital in one industry or sector, you are putting yourself at great risk. Stay away from this practice despite the promise of high returns. Even if you make some profits, they will be quite different as opposed to market performance.

Dividend investing is not exempted from market volatility. No one can surely know what will happen in the future, so it is not ideal to invest all your money in just one company or one sector.

Do you still remember the case of Enron? What about Lehman Brothers? Putting all your eggs in one basket can lead to disaster.

Let's say you decided to buy stocks from companies coming from different sectors. Even if one or two sectors are struggling, other sectors might be doing well. Hence, your portfolio will still grow.

You should avoid relying on one sector to grow your capital and receive dividend payouts. Your portfolio should be capable of sustaining unforeseen events because it is diversified.

As long as the stock market is there and companies are actively operating their businesses, there is no reason for your diversified portfolio to lose its value. Over the years, the stock market has been following an upward trend, but there are no indicators that this will go south anytime soon.

A well-balanced and diversified investment portfolio can help you distribute the risk and achieve your investment objectives. Building your portfolio starts with an understanding of the fundamental risk factors, which could affect the profitability and volatility of your dividend investments.

Risk Factors to Consider in Diversifying Your Portfolio

Diversifying your investment portfolio doesn't completely eliminate the risk in stock dividend investing. This practice only distributes the risk, so you can still grow your investments while receiving regular passive income.

Even if you diversify, you still need to understand several important risk factors that can affect your investments.

- The number of stock holdings
- The level of financial leverage for each stock
- The dynamics between holdings
- The market cap

These risk factors can significantly affect the performance of your investment portfolio, especially if the stock market is considered bearish.

For example, let's assume that half of your portfolio is composed of stocks from small-cap energy companies with high leverage. As the price of oil increases, your investment appreciates significantly with tolerable volatility.

Some investors would usually cite their "investment skills" and not luck if the results are favorable. However, the movement was nothing more than a gamble on the energy sector and good market conditions.

If the price of oil falls and there are fewer units available for small-cap companies, the heavily invested portfolio will substantially lose its value.

The primary point of building your investment portfolio is to distribute the factor bets that are beyond your control, and focus your returns on the performance of each company.

The Number of Share Holdings

The majority of lucrative investment companies are maintaining portfolios that are regarded as concentrated. For example, the highly successful Berkshire Hathaway has several holdings that stay within 10% of the total value of its stock portfolio.

The CEO of the company, Warren Buffett, is firm in investing in the best stocks on the market.

But you may not have the connections, insights, and resources of a big investment company to stick to a highly concentrated investment strategy.

Hence, it's recommended for private dividend investors to distribute their bets over a reasonable range of different stocks to minimize the risk of losing your investment capital.

A low number of shareholdings could increase the probability of your portfolio to go wayward. So it is essential to figure out the right number of holdings that you must have so you can really take advantage of diversification.

So what is the ideal number of stockholdings to include in your dividend investment portfolio?

The American Association of Individual Investors (AAII) recommends the following:

> "Holding a single stock rather than a perfectly diversified portfoli
> increases annual volatility by roughly 30%...Thus, the single-stoc
> will experience annual returns that average a whopping 35% abov
> below the market - with some years closer to the market and som
> further from the market."

AAII also recommends the following general rule to reduce investment risk through diversification:

- 400 stocks - risk will be reduced down to 95%

- 100 stocks - risk will be reduced down to 90%

- 25 stocks - risk will be reduced down to 80%

Another group of stock market researchers discovered that a higher number of holdings is needed to distribute the risk during a financial recession. The correlation between the number of stocks and risk is often the highest during negative economic conditions.

The study concluded that in the US, holding an average of 55 stocks in a portfolio will decrease the risk by about 90%. But this number should be increased to 110 stocks during turbulent times.

Based on these studies, the ideal number of holdings is between 30 to 100 stocks. However, if you run the numbers, you must also consider other factors that are inherent to your financial condition such as the size of your investment portfolio, available resources for conducting due diligence, and the cost of trading.

A smaller portfolio is usually susceptible to the effects of trading costs. If you have a small portfolio, you may have to purchase dividend ETFs rather than individual stocks so you can quickly diversify your investment and reduce trading cost. If you own more positions, you need less time to conduct due diligence.

While this is still susceptible to individual circumstances, holding between 25 and 70 stocks can balance your portfolio considering the factors mentioned earlier. Focusing on higher-quality stocks with a restricted range of possible results could help you to reduce the risk and build a more focused investment.

If you prefer a portfolio composed of speculative stocks, you may follow the path towards diversification with around 60 holdings.

Some dividend investors prefer to roughly balance their investments because it is often difficult to determine which stocks will perform well in the long term. As you gain more experience, you will have your own insights on how much holdings you can include in your portfolio as well as the level of your risk tolerance.

Sectoral Diversification

Adding the ideal number of stocks in your portfolio doesn't automatically make it diversified.

There are dividend investors who end up with an unbalanced portfolio because they are following specific investing rules such as purchasing stocks with P/E ratio lower than 12 points or focusing on specific types of stocks like green technology companies or only consumer staples.

However, holding on to stocks with the same features will not help you maximize the advantages of diversification. More often than not, stocks that are from similar sectors are often sensitive to the same factors, and they also share the same residual risks.

If a shared factor-like interest rates or oil prices becomes unfavorable, your investment portfolio may significantly underperform. Choosing stocks from different sectors can help you in distributing the risk because it is quite unlikely that all sectors of the economy will struggle all at the same time.

Some experienced dividend investors prefer to invest a quarter of their capital into one sector, then try to hold onto stocks with minimum overlap into the actual business operations.

Sadly, there's no fail-proof method that you can use to figure out which sectors would perform well in a specific period of time. Hence, it is important to diversify into the sector and industry levels.

But you must take note that diversifying based on sectors should not come at the expense of opposing principles of business valuation or exploring other sectors for new investments.

For instance, the S&P 500 index is composed of at least 7% companies that are under the consumer staples sector. But this doesn't recommend that you must choose stocks from this sector alone.

Furthermore, you should avoid diversifying into a sector that is way beyond your expertise. If you want to invest in a sector, don't skip due diligence and consult your colleagues who have the experience and expertise in investing in this particular sector.

Many dividend investors who are conservative in their stance have limited investments in tech companies because the pace in this sector is quite rapid, as opposed to more established sectors like finance. It is often difficult to predict which tech companies will still exist in the decades to come.

Chapter Takeaways

In this chapter, we have learned the following:

- Diversifying your investment portfolio may mitigate the unsystematic risk events so the stocks that are performing well can counter the bad performance of other stocks.

- Dividend investing is not exempted from market volatility. No one can surely know what will happen in the future, so it is not ideal to invest all your money in just one company or one sector.

- Diversifying across businesses and sectors is essential for successful dividend investing.

- You should choose sectors that you are really comfortable with and always carefully assess each possible investment that you want to be included in your portfolio.

Choosing company stocks to invest with is one of the most exciting areas of dividend investing.

However, time will come that you have to let go of some of your stocks. How can you tell that it's time to sell your stocks?

Let's find out in the next chapter.

Chapter 9 - When Is the Best Time to Sell a Dividend Stock?

"I try to buy shares of unpopular companies when they look like roadkill and sell them when they've been polished up a bit." - Michael Burry

Most books on dividend investing highlight the process of choosing stocks to buy and strategies on building your portfolio.

The subject of selling your stocks is often ignored because most investors are more excited to buy than sell. Their minds are more focused on the revenues they could gain from dividend payouts and the possible growth of their holdings.

If you have to sell your holdings, it is either you don't see the stock performing well or you need to use the money so you have to cash out. Selling your property is not as exciting as buying.

Why Sell Your Dividend Stocks

Before we go to the question of "when to sell?" let's try to answer the question of "why sell?

There are three primary reasons why you may need to sell your stocks:

1. If you believe the stocks are about to lose significantly in the market

2. If you believe that the company has already lost its competitive advantage

3. If you have figured out that the stocks are already selling above fair value

It is best to sell stocks with P/E ratio of higher than 40 because it indicates that the stock is already underperforming.

For example, the image below from Compustat/Faceset charts the performance of stocks with high P/E ratios as opposed to stocks with lower values in a period of 35 years.

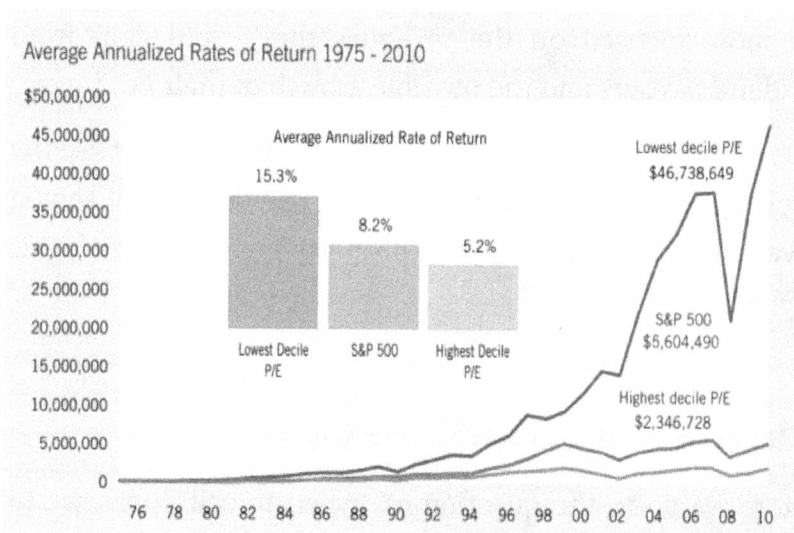

Average Annualized Rates of Return 1975 - 2010

Stocks with higher trade prices have significantly underperformed in the market. The regular range of P/E ratio is now used as a cut-off because this is the nearest valuation that the entire index has attained. A stock with a ratio of 40 indicates that it could be overvalued.

It's recommended to use regular range revenue figures rather than GAAP revenues. Try to stay away from selling stocks with P/E ratio of 40 because this means that the revenue is reduced by 50% usually because of temporary fluctuations in the market.

Also, stick to your high-cycle holdings even if they have a high P/E ratio. More often than not, the reduced profits at a given time are caused by the cyclical wave in the sector. Selling your overpriced stocks will shift your investments to a fair value that will provide you with dividend payouts and capital appreciation.

Aside from the numbers, another factor that you should always consider in selling your stock is the competitive advantage of the company.

Your passive income will be affected if the company suddenly decides to cancel or reduce the payouts.

Remember, the primary goal of holding high-quality dividend growth stocks is to make sure that your holdings will steadily grow over the years. It is not reasonable for a dividend investor to still hold onto stocks that are already not paying dividends.

Cutting or reducing dividend payouts sends a bad signal to dividend stock investors. It generally shows that the company is not capable anymore of sustaining the present cash flow.

This could even mean that the value proposition or the competitive advantage of the company has been significantly affected by disruptions, competition, or other factors.

Therefore, you should seriously consider selling the stocks of companies who have canceled their payouts.

Companies who have decided to permanently cancel their payouts generally provide minimal returns. Some stock analysts even argue that you are better off saving your money in the bank than holding on to stocks that are not growing and not providing payouts.

Check the Oppenheimer chart below, which demonstrates how dividend stocks have significantly outpaced stocks that stopped giving payouts.

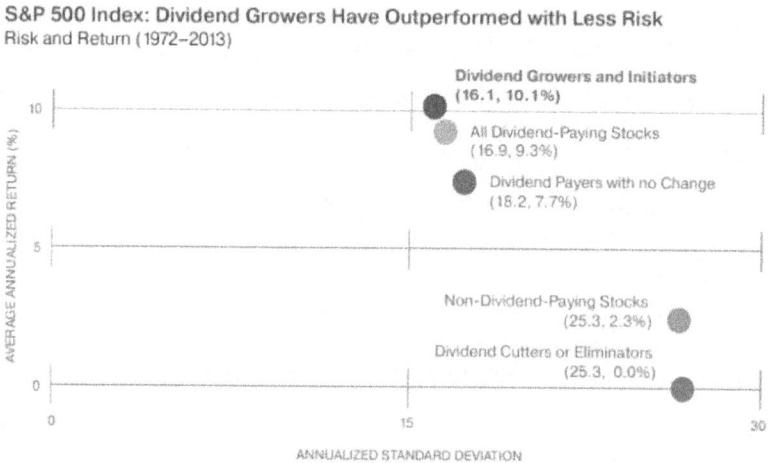

S&P 500 Index: Dividend Growers Have Outperformed with Less Risk
Risk and Return (1972–2013)

Dividend Growers and Initiators
(16.1, 10.1%)

All Dividend-Paying Stocks
(16.9, 9.3%)

Dividend Payers with no Change
(18.2, 7.7%)

Non-Dividend-Paying Stocks
(25.3, 2.3%)

Dividend Cutters or Eliminators
(25.3, 0.0%)

AVERAGE ANNUALIZED RETURN (%)

ANNUALIZED STANDARD DEVIATION

The Role of Ex-Dividend Date in Selling Dividend Stocks

As we have discussed in the first chapter of this book, you are not qualified to receive dividend payouts from your holdings if you sell before the ex-dividend date.

To freshen up your mind, the ex-dividend refers to the specific data that the company has assigned as the first day of trading without the payout privileges.

But here's an important thing that you should not forget: you are still qualified for payouts if you sell your stocks after the ex-dividend date.

To qualify for the payout, your name should be listed in the company's date of record, which is used to identify the shareholders of the company.

If you buy stocks today, your name will not automatically appear in the list of shareholders. It may take around at least 3 days before your name can be included.

Therefore, if the date of the record is September 15, you must buy the stocks on September 12 so you are still qualified for the payouts. This makes September 13 as the ex-dividend date because this is the date that directly follows the last date when you have received the payout.

The National Association of Securities Dealers monitors the process of recording the ex-dividend date of dividend-paying companies.

Chapter Summary

Selling your holdings is not as attractive as buying stocks to build your investment portfolio.

But in order to build something great, you need to understand the importance of trimming down the parts that don't fit in the design and function.

A dividend investment portfolio is designed to provide you with two things:

1. Regular passive income in the form of dividend payouts

2. Wealth accumulation through capital appreciation

If a particular stock doesn't fit into these two fundamental criteria, then there's no point holding it in.

In the final chapter, we will explore the importance of reinvesting your dividends to further accumulate your wealth.

Chapter 10 - Why Reinvest Your Dividends?

"When Warren Buffett invests in a company, he is conferring upon that company something very unique: his credibility."
- Bethany McLean

Amateur dividend investors are excited about the prospect of receiving cash payouts from their holdings.

Experienced dividend investors, on the other hand, don't cash out their dividends and instead reinvest them into the company.

Reinvesting your dividends is one of the best practices in stock dividend investing. Instead of cashing out, you can just reinvest your profits so you are gradually building your wealth.

Many dividend-issuing companies offer a Dividend Reinvestment Program or known as DRIP. This program will allow you to automatically reinvest your cash dividends into more shares.

One huge advantage of signing up for a DRIP account is the big savings you can get because you don't have to pay agency commission. So you can get a substantial discount if you purchase added shares through DRIP instead of buying from stock investment firms.

Remember, when dividend payouts are issued to shareholders, they are either distributed as direct deposit or a check sent to your home or office.

The shares that are purchased through a DRIP are typically sourced out from the own reserves of the business. Therefore, they are not offered publicly in the stock market, and they can only be redeemed directly through the company.

One point to consider though is the reporting of dividend as taxable income. When companies offer DRIP, you may set it up via brokerage as the majority of brokers facilitate reinvestment of dividends.

Types of Reinvestment Programs

Many dividend investors are into reinvestment programs. Therefore, more dividend companies are offering their own DRIPs.

But not all DRIPs are the same. Before you decide to sign up in any reinvestment program, you should be aware of the different types:

In-House

Most reinvestment programs are operated by companies as an in-house business activity. These are often handled by a particular division (typically Investor Relations) to take care of all aspects of the program.

But there are also companies that allow private investors to purchase stocks through a DRIP sign up so investors don't need to go through brokers.

Third-Party

Other companies outsource the management of their reinvestment plans.

Instead of running it in-house, they tap third-party agencies who employ transfer agents who often work on behalf of the company to handle all aspects of the reinvestment program.

Brokerage

Stockbrokers also offer reinvestment plans. Not all dividend companies have in-house DRIPs, and instead of outsourcing the program to external agencies, they would rather entrust the task to established stock brokerage firms.

But take note that brokerage firms earn revenue either through a fee paid by dividend companies or by taking a small percentage from the payout. Most stockbrokers are only offering DRIPs to investors who have existing accounts for commissioned stocks.

Why Companies Offer Reinvestment Programs?

Running reinvestment programs can provide a lot of benefits to companies that are regularly issuing dividends.

In general, if the shares are acquired from the company through a reinvestment scheme, this will generate more capital for the business.

Shareholders who signed up for reinvestment are less motivated to sell their stocks even if there are adverse movements in the market. Reinvested dividends are not as liquid as stocks purchased in the market.

Furthermore, experienced dividend investors easily recognize the role that their dividends play in the long-term growth of their portfolio.

Why Should You Reinvest Your Dividends Instead of Cashing Out?

There are several advantages of acquiring stocks through a DRIP. Basically, a reinvestment program can provide you with an easier way to buy more shares without the need to pay brokerage fees or commissions (unless you are buying from broker companies).

Many dividend companies are also offering stocks at a reduced rate through their own reinvestment programs. The discount may range between 1% to 10%. With this discount and zero commissions, the cost of buying dividend stocks through DRIP can be significantly lower as opposed to purchasing the stocks in the open market.

Moreover, the impact of DRIP in the accumulation of wealth is considered as the biggest benefit for dividend investors. By increasing your holdings, you are also increasing the payouts you can expect. You can then use the payouts to buy more shares.

In the long run, this strategy can easily boost your possible returns. You can even buy more shares if the share price falls. The long-term potential for capital gains also skyrockets.

What Are the Disadvantages of Reinvesting Your Dividends?

Reinvesting your dividends is not the ultimate solution in dividend investing. There are still several drawbacks that you should carefully review before you sign up for a DRIP.

Basically, dividend investors who focus on the dividend yield can easily see a disadvantage in the scheme because it falls on the minimal discretion on the price that you are paying to acquire the new stocks.

Under a reinvestment program, the acquisition will be immediate and will always follow the price that is established by the stock market despite the discount offered by the company.

This can be perceived by some investors as a disadvantage because it may be difficult for you to decline the reinvestment if you think that the price of the stock is overvalued. So always check if the reinvestment program has clear provisions on what you can do if you want to decline the offer and you prefer to cash out the dividends.

Just take note that the purchased stocks through a DRIP will be acquired at any phase of the market cycle. There will be instances that the shares are at an all-time low, and there will always be cases that they are overpriced.

Chapter Takeaways

In this final chapter, we have learned the following:

- Reinvesting your dividends through an automatic DRIP offered by companies can help you easily grow your holdings.

- Reinvesting will save you time as you don't need to call each company just to tell them that you want your dividends to be reinvested.

- Reinvesting will save you money because if you buy the shares in-house, you don't need to pay broker fees and commission.

- The convenience of signing up for a DRIP should not encourage you to skip due diligence.

- Always review the fine print of any reinvestment program you are offered.

Conclusion

Congratulations on finishing the beginner's guide to dividend investing!

Hopefully, you are now armed with know-how and insights so you can start building the investment portfolio that will provide you with regular passive income and potential capital growth.

But take note that this book should not end your journey towards learning more about dividend investing.

Reading a book is easy. Executing the strategies you have learned is another thing.

The stock market is an exciting yet messy financial market. But if you study it well and follow through the hustle, you can definitely win the game.

My intention is to help you decide if dividend investing is the right game plan for you, and I hope this book has provided you with the knowledge, confidence, and the resolve you need.

Thank you

Before you go, I just wanted to say thank you for purchasing my book.

You could have picked from dozens of other books on the same topic but you took a chance and chose this one.

So, a HUGE thanks to you for getting this book and for reading all the way to the end.

Now I wanted to ask you for a small favor. **Could you please consider posting a review on the platform? Reviews are one of the easiest ways to support the work of authors.**

This feedback will help me continue to write the type of books that will help you get the results you want. So if you enjoyed it, please let me know.

www.ingramcontent.com/pod-product-compliance
Lightning Source LLC
Chambersburg PA
CBHW071417210326
41597CB00020B/3543